ALASKA BEARS
Stirred and Shaken

JAKE JACOBSON
Alaska's Favorite Real Life Wilderness Storyteller

PUBLICATION CONSULTANTS
Because We Believe In The Power Of Authors
PO Box 221974 Anchorage, Alaska 99522-1974
books@publicationconsultants.com—www.publicationconsultants.com

ISBN 978-1-59433-706-2

eBook ISBN: 978-1-59433-707-9

Library of Congress Catalog Card Number: 2017937558

Copyright 2017 Jake Jacobson

—First Edition—

All rights reserved, including the right of reproduction in any form, or by any mechanical or electronic means including photocopying or recording, or by any information storage or retrieval system, in whole or in part in any form, and in any case not without the written permission of the author.

J.P. "Jake" Jacobson
Alaska Master Guide #54
PO Box 1313
Kodiak, Alaska 99615
website: www.huntfish.us/
email: huntfish@ak.net

Manufactured in the United States of America.

My friend and sometime hunting companion, Craig Boddington wrote the foreword for my first book, *ALASKA HUNTING: Earthworms to Elephants*.

Patrick McManus, Bob Penfold, and Dr. Larry Gates, all of whom hunted or fished with me, wrote forewords for my second publication, *ALASKA TALES: Laughs and Surprises*.

I considered noting on the cover of my third book, *ALASKA FLYING: Surviving Incidents and Accidents* that neither the Wright brothers, Charles Lindberg nor Chuck Yeager wrote forwards for that book, but I decided against mentioning that.

For this book, I thought it might be a good thing to clarify that neither Daniel Boone, Davy Crockett, Ben Lilly nor W.D.M "Karamojo" Bell wrote a foreword - but I decided to not put that on the front cover.

Other books by Jake Jacobson are:
ALASKA HUNTING: Earthworms to Elephants,
ALASKA TALES: Laughs and Surprises and
ALASKA FLYING: Surviving Incidents & Accidents

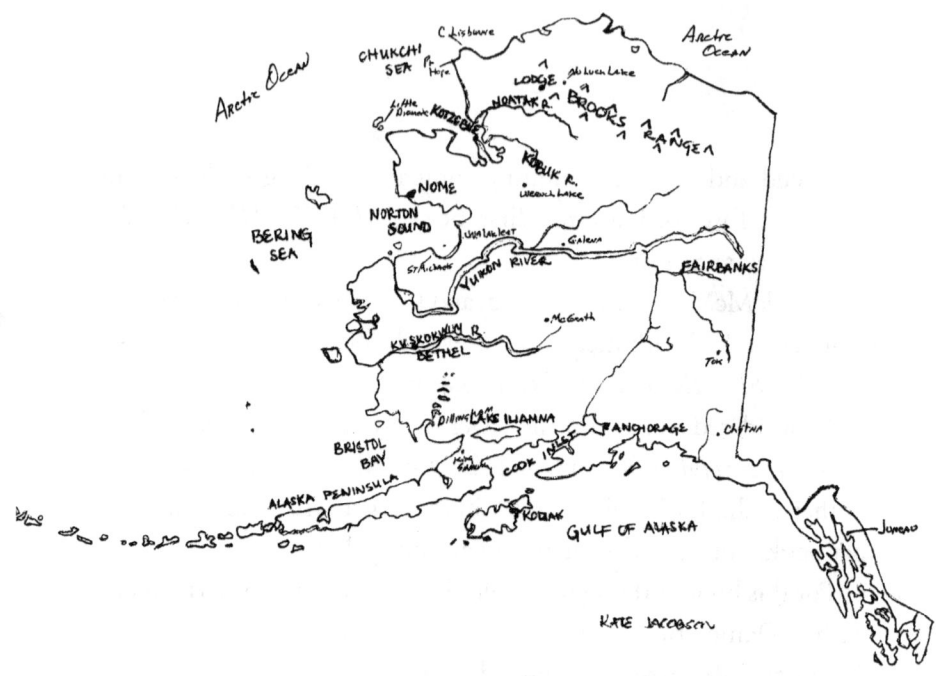

Map credit: Kate Jacobson

Contents

Testimonials 6

Introduction: Alaska Bears ... 11

My First Bears in Alaska 25

1968: A Black Bear
Encounter While
Carrying Fish 29

In Pursuit of the Ice Bear 33

Three Bears Before Lunch 37

Black Bear Uses 45

Spring Grizzly Hunt
on Snowshoes 51

My Sister,
Pat, Takes a Grizzly 59

Huge Grizzly at
Close Range 71

Grizzlies-Live Capture 81

Always Best to Hunt
with a Reliable Partner 87

Cold Steel by
the Outhouse 93

Big Grizzly by Bow 99

Three Dutchmen Take
Three Big Bears 111

Cabin
Protective Measures 133

A Toklat Grizzly
Comes A'Knockin' 139

A Chronicle of
the Second Bear
Break-In 147

2000, Greg Fischer's
Mauling 169

Greg Fisher's Return
To Trail Creek 193

A Weekend in Kodiak 203

It Takes a Girl to
Kill a Grizzly 213

The Rogue Sow 219

"PULL" Another Bear 227

A Toklat Grizzly
in Heavy Snow 235

Testimonials

ALASKA BEARS: Stirred and Shaken

Following are a few reviews from my first three books.

WHAT OTHERS SAY: In Amazon book reviews.

ALASKA HUNTING: *Earthworms to Elephants*

Greg, Soldotna, Ak.

As a long time resident, I love Alaska and all the adventure that it offers. I also enjoy reading about the adventures of others. As a result, I have several hundred books related to hunting, trapping and flying in Alaska.

The author's collection of stories is as good as it gets. He writes in a descriptive and down to earth manner. Unless you have experienced it, it is hard to grasp the intoxicating nature of hunting and flying in Alaska's remote backcountry. The author does an excellent job of taking you along for the ride.

Additionally, his stories illustrate the depth and knowledge he has gained in over 45 years of guiding in Alaska. Each chapter and story holds your interest and you find yourself wanting to read on to the next. It is obvious that the author is an accomplished outdoorsman and knowledgeable about the species he pursues.

In conclusion, I give this book a five star rating - you will enjoy it. I suspect the author has lots more stories. I hope so, as I am looking forward to a second book.

ALASKA HUNTING: Earthworms to Elephants
Dr. Larry Gates, Salem, Oregon

Henry David Thoreau wrote, "most men lead lives of quiet desperation, and go to the grave with the song still in them." Sometimes, a man leads an interesting life. Infrequently, one leads a consequential life. Rarely the two come together. If the rest of us are very lucky, that man is also a gifted natural storyteller. Over the course of a lifetime, Jake Jacobson, dentist, outfitter and guide, entrepreneur and family man, has polished his stories like the jade and petrified mammouth ivory he has lifted from the Alaskan outback. He has entertained generations of hunting clients in the cluttered comfort of his arctic lodge. Now, those stories can reach a wider audience in this volume. All that is missing is the smell of caribou stew and trail creek berry bread wafting in from the kitchen.

Jake Jacobson has produced a beautiful little gem of a book. It is a collection of vignettes that are alternatingly moving, perplexing, heartwarming, and hysterical. A grandson experiences the magic of a first hunting trip. A famous hunting author is the butt of an elaborate practical joke. A former senator is chased from camp at rifle point. The writing style is conversational and engaging. A wealth of black and white photographs illustrate the stories.

I'm tempted to compare Jake to Peter Capstick Hathaway, Robert Ruark, or Patrick F. McManus, but that would be unfair. He's James P. "Jake" Jacobson, DMD, Alaska Master Guide #54. He is one of a kind, and this book guarantees that he will not go to the grave with the song still in him!

ALASKA TALES: Laughs and Surprises
Craig Boddington

I have been fortunate to spend time in the Alaskan wilderness with Jake Jacobson ... aside from being a very genuine Alaskan legend not just as an outdoorsman, but one of the early "flying dentists" serving Arctic communities — he's a real character and truly a funny guy. Read the "laughs and surprises" of his Alaska Tales, and you'll feel like you're seeing his wild Alaska ... and laughing along with him.

ALASKA TALES: Laughs and Surprises
Ron Rico, Colorado

A thoroughly enjoyable read! What a refreshing departure from the ho-hum of so much written material! This collection of short stories related to Alaska hunting details various aspects of modern Professional Hunting in our northernmost state. It focuses on dealing with the occasional absurdity of human nature, the vagaries and idiosyncrasies of people, including guests, guides and peripheral personnel. Jake dissects events, locating the humorous aspects of what might otherwise be completely negative scenarios. He sees the humor, sometimes adding to it, and makes the best of situations, however bizarre they might be. Legends and superstitions are explored and in some cases, exploited. If the reader is looking for relief from everyday "Great White Hunter" stories - give this publication a read. It will lighten your load and give you relief from the doldrums of average, everyday existence. This is the author's second publication …… and I hope he writes more. My ribs hurt from laughing

ALASKA FLYING: Surviving Incidents and Accidents
David A. Johnson, Tennessee

Once in a great while, one finds a book that's entertaining, educational and fun to read. This is it! For anyone desiring to own and operate a bush airplane in Alaska or any other large wilderness area, anywhere in the world, this book is a necessity. Jake, through innumerable episodes and incidences, will educate the potential new pilot or inquisitive passenger of a bush aircraft, to be aware of the adventures and potential dangers awaiting those who climb aboard a bush aircraft. I was one of those persons ensconced in the back seat of Jake's airplane, as a ADF&G biologist, between 1977-1984. Early on I found it advantages to always give the pilot his discretion and found it much better to never challenge the pilot into extraneous or challenging flight or landing conditions that would endanger pilot, passenger and aircraft. There will always be a better and safer time.

ALASKA FLYING: Surviving Incidents and Accidents
Utah State Aggie

God has a special purpose for Jake Jacobson. There is no other explanation for his being here to grace us with "Alaska Flying: Surviving Incidents and Accidents", the latest installment of Jake's Alaska series.

Jake is a terrific storyteller. If you have read his other books, Alaska Hunting: Earthworms to Elephants, and Alaska Tales: Laughs and Surprises, you already know that. He benefits from priceless material. Jake's life, by chance and choice, is a cornucopia of the absurd, comical, heartwarming, and bizarre. He has a natural storyteller's gift. Do a little experiment; close your eyes and let your favorite hunting companion read you one of Jake's stories. You'll feel the warmth of the campfire on your hands, the arctic breeze in your hair, and hear the gentle burbling of Trail Creek in the background. Jake brings every vignette to life.

As good as Jake's previous efforts have been, this book may be his best effort yet. The other two books are character studies, filled with the quirky denizens of the last frontier. This book has a much narrower cast, essentially Jake and his planes. Jake has an almost intimate relationship with his planes. He writes about his favorite, "21 Poppa", as "feel[ing] like an extension of my own body...... That Cub, to me, is a bit like one's first kiss – memorable, unique, and never to be repeated." This is certainly Jake's most personally revealing book. In writing about those planes, and the moments they have liberated him, sustained him, and brought him close to death, Jake shows more of his own character than he has in his previous works.

As I said, I truly believe that God has a special purpose for Jake. Jake is a superb pilot, as I know from personal experience. The interior of Alaska is littered with the bones of superb pilots. Many of the stories in this book are brushes with death and disaster. No one could do what Jake has done for 45 years without being held, as he puts it, "in the palm of God's hand". Do yourself a favor. Read the book and see if I'm not right.

ALASKA FLYING: Surviving Incidents and Accidents
Richard Dobson, Texas

Every red blooded American hunter has dreamed of big game pursuit in the great wilderness of Alaska. Not only does Jake's book take you there, you experience it through the eyes of a true bush pilot. You're there in the cockpit with him, as he marvels at the splendor of our last frontier. Bush flying in Alaska is not for the weak of heart, and you ride with Jake as he wins, loses, and sometimes gets away by the skin of his teeth. A great story teller for sure, you'll leap from one adventure to the next until there are no more pages to read.

Introduction: Alaska Bears

When I was still a child, using my BB gun, then later the single shot .22 caliber rifle my Dad gave me, I dreamed of hunting bears ... and I imagined hunting just about everything else.

Bears, lions, and other wild beasts of aggressive nature and potential danger fascinated me somehow differently than did ungulates and lagomorphs (rabbits - which, by the way, are not rodents). Stories of the courage of Daniel Boone and Davy Crockett - "killin' them thar bars" excited me in some ancient, primordial way. In my youthful dreams, no doubt common to young fellows back in the days when every boy carried a pocket knife, but I'm not so sure about kids today, I saw myself standing firm and unflinching in the face of a huge oncoming bear bent on doing me damage. But having only one shot, I held my fire until the right moment. And I never was victimized by the bear in any of my daydreams or nightmares - or to date in actual encounters with hundreds of bruins in my fifty years in Alaska, thank God!

During my sixteenth through eighteenth summers I lived with my uncle Stan who was foreman for a large ranch in Montana. I longed for an opportunity to dispatch a black bear as I protected the cattle and horses of the ranch. But it never happened. My only encounter which could have led to taking a bear evaporated, because I did not have my rifle handy, but fortunately I had my Brownie Box camera, so I snapped a black and white photograph of the critter.

As I was making my way to a remote Alaska village in 1967, with my non-resident ten dollar tag in my pocket, my dreams of killing a bear were fulfilled. In fact I killed three black bears within about thirty minutes in the course of traveling from Cordova to Tatitlek. But there was nothing very exciting or dramatic about any of it.

The next time I killed a bear, it too, was a black bear, but I killed it with my .357 pistol as I was returning to my pick-up with some fresh salmon.

I had been shaken and that was a stirring experience.

In the past fifty years I have participated in killing bears of all the North American species, Polar bears, Brown bears, Grizzlies and Black bears.

From my pre-teen years I have always wanted to know as much about animals as I could learn, especially animals that I was dealing with or longed to hunt some day, so here's some of what I've learned.

Differences in Bears

Each species of North American bears has it's peculiarities, differences, and vulnerabilities. All are of the order *Carnivora*, yet all are actually omnivores - like pigs and people - they eat both meat and plant food. The percentage of meat versus plant nutrients in their diet varies with species of bears and is seasonally influenced. Polar bears consume the highest percentage of meat and fat, with seal blubber preferred. The other species of bears' diets are determined by their access to fish, beach food, carrion, berries, garbage, and other food sources. All bears relish carrion whether it's spoiled, maggot-infested, or fresh.

Determining the age of bears is done by making a cross section of a vestigial premolar from the mandible, or lower jaw. Once the tooth is cut into a thin section, the differential growth in tooth cementum can be seen - similar to tree rings. The growth rings apparently are due to the retarded growth and slowed metabolism of the animal during hibernation. Wild bears do not usually live as long as their cousins in captivity.

Alaskan Polar bears, with the exception of pregnant females, do not hibernate like land bears, so the annual rings are not so distinct. This makes the accurate determination of age of Polar bears difficult. I suspect that reliable aging of bears in warm desert country might be similarly compromised.

All bears are intelligent, but polar bears (*Ursus maritimus*) seem to be the most intelligent and aggressive of their Order. Once while hunting on the ice in 1971 I was waiting with a guest hunter for a shot at a large male which was closely following a female. We figured we were hidden in the ice of a pressure ridge, but the boar spotted us. After once looking directly

Introduction: Alaska Bears

1959 photo taken from the truck window, Brownie Box camera in hand, but no rifle.

at us, the bear did not again make eye contact, but it definitely edged closer to us, cross-stepping deliberately toward our position. I've never seen any other bear act like that, but I was reminded of politicians and their methods of deceptively leading us to think they plan something other than what they actually intend to do. I realized we had become the targets of a highly intelligent adversary - which also all too often, applies to politicians.

While in a wall tent at a whaling camp on the ice near Point Hope I was alerted to a medium sized Polar bear sneaking toward the tent. A young boy had just delivered some fresh doughnuts and the bear seemed to be stalking him. One of the local fellows shot that bear and its meat - all but

Showing no fear, this Polar bear came right in as I took pictures.

the liver - went into the stew pot. The hide went to the village for women to flesh, tan and make useful.

Two young men to whom I had provided dental care were killed and eaten by Polar bears on the northwest Alaskan coast.

Brown and Grizzly bears are now both classified as *Ursus arctos*. They carry nearly the same DNA, and commonly interbreed where their artificially designated range boundaries overlap, but their size and habits differ greatly. The larger than average grizzly bears of Norton Sound could well be classified as brown bears due to their salmon rich diet and relatively mild winters. The massive brownies have a diet rich in salmon and enjoy longer periods of warmer weather, which results in their larger size.

The grizzlies of the interior and far north spend more time and effort making a living from their often hungry country, therefore depending more on grasses which are far less nutritious than salmon. The grizzlies living in colder regions also spend much more time in hibernation - a period of minimal growth. Perhaps their more difficult way of life have led to their fierce nature, awe-inspiring reputation, and the old name, *Ursus horribilis*.

Grizzlies, especially those living in the interior areas, have to scratch a lot harder for a living than the coastal bears do, and as a consequence, they have much larger ranges or territories. One female Grizzly I was involved with capturing, radio collaring, and tracking, had a home range of over four hundred miles in circumference. That is an exceptionally large chunk of territory for any land bear.

A blond Grizzly passed just below us near the main stream on Trail Creek

In the Kodiak Archipelago, with its rain throughout the year, many Brown bears spend little, if any time in a den. Some biologists estimate that as high as thirty percent of Kodiak bears do not den at all. Given their longer time in the sun, they are able to flower to maximum size.

Hunting

Successfully hunting bears is aided by exploitation of their particular vulnerabilities and habits.

Airborne Polar bear guided hunts focused on open leads in the offshore sea ice of the Bering and Chukchi Seas - usually many miles from shore and often closer to the Siberian shore than Alaskan beaches. Today Polar bears in Alaska are legally hunted only by coastal dwelling Alaska Natives along the shores of the frozen Arctic seas. Some remote areas in Canada and Greenland also provide opportunities to hunt the ice bear.

Brown bears are most commonly hunted near salmon streams, especially in areas that have late fall runs of fish. When fish vacate the area, many of the bears move back to the berry patches and consume grasses along with the little wild fruits which have a high sugar content. The beaches provide a menu change twice daily with the tides, so local bears frequent the beaches at most times of the year.

On spring hunts in mountainous country it pays to watch snowy hillsides and snow chutes, as bears often slide down those areas. Apparently they're having fun, as they often climb back up and slide again.

A Kodiak bear suddenly encountered while on a deer hunt. My son, Martin Shroyer took this photo.

With Black bears, if salmon streams are nearby, that's the ideal place to hunt them, as well as ocean beaches, but away from such protein rich places, berry patches draw the *Ursus americaus* during autumn.

But with any type of bear, their acute sense of smell may lure them away from their normal haunts if they detect carrion.

Human Contact

Most bear and human contacts result in the bear charging off to get away from the strange looking and odd smelling people, but sometimes, unfortunately for the bears and people, inter-specie contacts lead to conflicts and some have dire consequences.

It's generally agreed that the best way to survive an attack by a Grizzly or Brown bear is to play dead. If the human under attack does not resist, the bear will most often depart without killing the person,

We counted over forty bears feeding on a whale in Old Kaguyak Bay on Kodiak Island.

although the individual is commonly scalped when the bear tries to bite through the skull. Other painful, serious injuries are common in bear attacks, as well.

Most experts agree that a human attacked by a Black bear should put up his or her best fight, as the Black bear intends to eat the *Homo sapiens* it has engaged.

There are not enough reports of Polar bear attacks on humans to result in a consensus on how to react, but common sense and the few instances I am aware of, lead me to recommend the strongest possible resistance - and one should hope to be able to use a big gun.

On the Table

When I first went to Kodiak Island in 1967, the school janitor from Old Harbor invited me to accompany him and another man on a bear hunt one Sunday. We took his little wooden skiff to Barling Bay and they harvested a Brown bear. Back in those days there were no deer, hares or other land meat animals that far south on Kodiak Island. Locals ate the bears they killed. So I got a taste of bear stew. It was well prepared and delicious, but since then, the brown bears I have taken or been involved with displayed an unappetizing odor of rotten fish and I've not consumed much brown bear meat since.

In the Iliamna Lake area as well as the Kotzebue country, on autumn hunts I always saved black bear meat for roasts and stews. Those berry-fed beasts are mighty fine eating and their fat makes a wonderful gravy.

Most polar bear guides and hunters did not bring in any meat, but I brought back at least the hams of the bear I took and that of bears taken by people I had helped. Only once was the flesh not palatable, but that was because the cook, unfamiliar with - and a bit fearful of the meat, used too much garlic on the roast. It was like an Arizona jack rabbit that an aunt of mine roasted with a gross overdose of garlic. Awful!

The grizzly bears from northwest Alaska which have not been feeding on fish in the fall are primarily grass and berry-fed and we enjoy tender roasts and great stews every year from their flesh. It tastes a lot like beef in flavor and it's always tender. Once we had corn fed grizzly, which I detail in another story. Not many people get to do that!

Shooting

My first wife, Mae, preferred a .270 for shooting black and grizzly bears and I've had some guest hunters that used that caliber, but I prefer our guests to bring a thirty caliber rifle for bears.

I used a .300 Winchester magnum on polar bears and found it to be adequate, as it is for all Alaskan big game. I use my own hand loaded 200 grain Hornaday bullets. The heavier bullet travels a bit slower but is less deflected by wind and results in less blood shot meat that the 150 or 180 grain missiles, making it ideal in my view as an all purpose load, for use on meat animals as well as bears.

Some reputable guides insist on larger caliber rifles for Brown bears, including .338,.375 and on up to .416 Rigby.

It's far more important where the bear is struck by the bullet than the type of bullet, caliber, or weight. Discussions go on endlessly regarding what is enough gun, type of bullet, etc. I recommend that each hunter use what works best in his rifle and in his hands. Where to aim depends on the bear's position. For a broadside shot I recommend aiming for the front shoulder. Commonly a bear will try to bite the place it is shot, giving the hunter an opportunity to feed it more lead.

A three year old cub showing the fading collar. ULRICH HERBST FOTO

Colors

Polar bears are ... well white, if not discolored from blood, blubber or other parts of a recent meal.

Brown and Grizzly bears vary in color from nearly black to a creamy white. Often cubs show a collar of lighter fur until age three or so.

Black bears are most commonly black, often with a small white patch on the chest, but various shades of the cinnamon color phases are seen, especially west of the Mississippi River. In Alaska the Glacier, or Blue bear is a unique color phase of *Ursus americanus* found on rare occasions throughout its range, but most frequently in the Yakutat area.

The other white bear, *Ursus americanus kermodei*, is found on some islands on the coast of British Columbia. I read that approximately ten percent of this subspecies carry a cream-colored coat. Biologists believe the color is due to a recessive gene. Perhaps such a genetic peculiarity explains the color of cinnamon and blue bears as well.

A black bear mother can produce a non-black bear cub in any of the color phases. This is similar to the three major color phases - silver, cross, and red - of the American Red Fox (*Vulpes vulpes*).

Mating

On several occasions I have been witness to grizzly bears mating. I used binoculars - not a peep hole. A boar may remain close to a sow for several days, copulating multiple times. I have seen a boar remain on the back of the sow for more than twenty minutes after the pelvic thrusts ceased, which I think is due to them being "hung up", such as is commonly seen with canines. I believe any animal with a baculum, oosic (the Inupiat word), or *os penis* remains in penetration of the female for a prolonged time. That is likely the purpose of that additional bone in species so endowed - or blessed - and perhaps plays an important part in the success of the boar's sperm reaching the egg. At least while hung up, no other boar's sperm can get to the ovum. The route is blocked, or plugged.

Recently I read in a scientific paper stating that female bears have a homologous bone called a baubellum or *os clitoridis*, but I've never noticed one. On the next big female we take, I plan to probe for one. I assume that is just a vestigial bone of no known purpose.

But to take the discussion of this mysterious bone a bit further, the *os clitoridis* has been found in a variety of rodents, carnivores, and primates - but not humans - while marmots, seals, cats, bats, bears, and more have some sort of bone beneath the clitoris. These curious little bones vary in shape with each species. In some ground squirrels it is shaped like a flared spoon with protruding spurs, while in other squirrels it may twist, taper, and flare in species- specific ways. Baubellem and baculum are homologous - they're essentially the same bone.

Regarding the male bear's baculum, it is often put to use as a stir-stick for cocktails. I wonder what useful purpose could be found for the baubellum - perhaps a nose or ear ring or other body adornment?

Medicine

When I was hunting polar bears, many of the old-time guides carefully removed the gall bladder after tying off its main duct with a piece of string. Those bladders were then sold to Chinese buyers for about three hundred dollars, who, it was reported, later peddled them for up to ten times that amount. Apparently the gall bladder of any bear was approximately equally effective, but the buyers in Hong Kong and Macao preferred those of polar bears.

Some traditional Asian medicines use the contents of bear gallbladders -bile - to treat a number of human ailments, such as liver disease, convulsions, diabetes, high fevers, and heart disease. While there is scientific evidence that supports the value of bear gall for remedies, some synthetic substances are equally effective.

In the United States, thirty-four states ban all trade in bear galls and bile, but five states allow the trade. In 1984 Alaska banned the sale of bear galls, but the sale of paws was not forbidden. The feet have a small amount of delicate meat between the pads and are considered a delicacy, fetching a high price in high-scale oriental restaurants,.

In my experience the size of the gall bladder (containing from half a cup to two cups of bile) is not directly related to the size or age of the bear. Some large bears have small galls and vice versa.

In 1977 my wife and I went to Singapore, Hong Kong and other places in the orient. I had been saving and drying bear galls for years due to the lack of a handy buyer, so I took several on that trip. But we were unknown to the owners of medicine shops and were therefore unable to sell the galls, as the potential buyers suspected we might be trying to palm pig galls off on them. When we returned, I sold my batch of galls to the only buyer I could locate in Anchorage.

Since the ban on sale of gall bladders in Alaska I still save as many as I can - which is not illegal - and give them to orientals, along with the feet. Better to do someone a good deed than waste a precious commodity, I figure. I have never got anything back for those bear parts, but I do not expect anything from merely doing a good deed. Somebody benefits, if only by putting a smile on their face.

When my own gall bladder was removed in 2009 I asked that it be saved for me, but the surgeon told me it was so badly scarred, she wanted to keep it for a instructional piece. I'd had gall stone attacks for over ten years which probably led to the scarring. So, I let the surgeon keep my troublesome body part.

Senses

SMELL: The most impressive of bears senses is that of their sense of smell. I've read that bears have thirty, forty or one hundred times the olfactory

ALASKA BEARS   Stirred and Shaken

A large gall bladder, and from a medium sized grizzly, by gally!

acuity of humans, but whatever the real number may be, their noses are far more accurate and useful than are our own. I believe all predators sense of smell is so much greater than that of humans, we really can't accurately gage or appreciate it. Suffice it to say that we humans should be aware of this vast difference and pay attention to the wind when in bear country.

HEARING: The ears of adult brown, grizzly, and polar bears are not so outstanding as those of many of their prey species, and big ears usually indicate an acute auditory capability, but bears do hear quite well. I've seen this demonstrated often enough by hunting companions whose voices spooked bears from several hundred yards away.

SIGHT: It is generally thought that bears, like porcine critters (pigs) are myopic and do not see well at a distance, but I've seen the contrary on many occasions. The large male polar bear that picked me and a hunter out while we thought we were well hidden in an icy pressure ridge wearing white parkas certainly displayed better than 20:20 vision. In 2000, Plumb Bob and I were spotted by a grizzly at over three hundred fifty yards as we sat in camouflage clothing on a hillside well below the skyline. I have observed many more demonstrations of the good eyesight of bears in the past fifty years. So I think bears see very well at long distances.

Individual bears of each species have personalities, if you're around them long enough to notice. Some are aggressive, others not so much, but any bear can turn gnarly, most any day, so that should be on your mind, lest a bear's bad day make yours a worse day.

But, enjoyable as it is, bear hunting has never been my favorite pursuit. Among all the species of animals I have hunted, my favorites are those I began chasing after for the table way back more than sixty-five years ago—rabbits or hares, and deer.

So I guess I'm one of those souls stuck in time. I'm still basically a meat hunter.

My First Bears In Alaska

I shot my first bears in Alaska in September, 1967. It wasn't especially exciting. I'd been weathered in at Cordova, en route via float plane to the native village called Tatitlik which was up toward Valdez.

After several days of sitting out of the rain in the old Parmeter hotel, reading and playing cribbage or pinochle with others stuck by the same meteorological conditions, one afternoon the weather seemed to improve, so I walked down to the air taxi office to find their two float planes loading up with sheep hunters to drop off in the Wrangel Mountains. The hunters had arrived in Cordova a day or so after my dental assistant and me, so I mentally questioned the priorities of the operator. It became apparent to me that our plane load of two passengers and several trunks of equipment might be put off indefinitely, as the trips to the remote drop off camps were much more lucrative for the owner of the flying business. Also the hunters' time was limited, and accessing their drop-off strips was far more unsure than going to our destination. In those days with no airport at Tatitlek or most other remote coastal villages, float planes landed in the ocean and taxied to the beach to off load passengers and freight. The operator told me that he would call me as soon as he could take us to the village, which was only about a half hour away by float plane.

As I headed back to the hotel, it occurred to me that the down time we had already experienced exceeded the time I needed to take care of the school children in Tatitlik, and that soon the overall expense in lost time and travel money was going to potentially keep some other village from getting their annual dental field trip. I had a strictly fixed budget with which to service many rural villages that fall. And I was responsible for monitoring the expenses.

Main street in Cordova, Alaska CORDOVA HISTORICAL SOCIETY

I stopped in a small cafe for a cup of coffee and overheard two fellows discussing taking their seiner up to Valdez. I moved from the counter to their table and asked the strangers if I could join them. They nodded affirmatively.

The older fellow introduced himself and his deck hand. (I'll call him Arne and his partner Rolf.) Explaining my situation, I offered to examine their teeth and perform whatever operative and light surgical procedures they might need, once I got set up in Tatitlik, which was on their way to Valdez, in exchange for a boat ride to the village. And furthermore, once the clinic was set up, they would be my first patients.

They said that sounded like a fine deal, as they were headed that way, and we could depart in about an hour.

My assistant was in her hotel room taking a nap, so I told her we had to hurry to be on the street to meet the two fellows with their pick-up truck and be taken to their boat.

We were on the boardwalk with all our gear in forty-five minutes.

We loaded the the 42 foot seiner and cast off the lines.

We were underway, finally.

I'd never been on a boat like that one before, and was really intrigued with it all. It had radar, an oil stove for cooking and cabin heat. Tight little bunks were in the forecastle and all was well kept and clean. It was not at all like what I'd heard about most "dirty little fishing boats". A small plywood skiff was towed behind for going ashore or to another boat.

Sea conditions were a little rough, and my assistant was not too keen on this mode of transportation in the first place, but she handled it well. While underway the skipper told me that he thought it best we anchor up for the night in a sheltered cove, then get an early start in the morning. That sounded like a good idea to me.

It was early September and silver salmon were jumping in the bay, prior to making their runs up the creeks.

We saw several Black Bears near the mouths of the creeks and other bruins strolled close to the beach. The bears were catching and feeding on the fish. I had my fishing pole, as well as a rifle and shotgun in a wooden case, so the skipper asked if I'd like to shoot a bear.

"Sure," I said.

We three men boarded the small wooden skiff and silently rowed toward the nearest bear. The water was coming in after an big low tide. We entered a narrow tidal gut and continued up that waterway which kept us about four feet below the level of the bank where one of the bears was stripping a fish. At about seventy-five yards I leveled my rifle on the neck just behind the head and squeezed off a shot, which dropped the bear - stone dead in it's tracks.

At the sound of my shot, another bear jumped up on the bank about twenty yards from the first. Rolf hollered, "There's another one" and stood up in the boat aiming his rifle. This commotion caused the second bear to turn and run toward the tree line, Rolf shot, but hit the bear in the guts, then as he attempted to lever another round into the chamber, his rifle jammed.

"Shoot him, I'm jammed !" he yelled.

I led the running bear a little for the quartering shot and broke his neck, which sent him on a nose dive into the muck. Now bears were appearing all over the flats, most seemed dumbstruck, but some were hightailing it for the timber. My assistant, talking it all in from the boat, said she counted 11 Black Bears within about 300 yards of us in the skiff.

Arne said, "Vell, ya may as well get anudder one, vile we're here." Rolf, whose rifle apparently had a defective extractor, was still trying to pick his jammed round out of the barrel, so I got up on the bank and took a broadside shot at the largest bear I could see and broke it's back, then put a second round into its chest as it struggled to get up.

This was some bear hunting, I thought. I had longed to take a black bear in Montana, but an opportunity had never come my way.

The tide was coming in, which allowed us to row the skiff up the little tidal guts, and close enough to each of the three carcasses to just roll them to the edge of the waterway and into the boat. The hides had plenty of mud on them, but it was the easiest game packing in which I had ever had the pleasure of participating.

We were back to the anchored seiner in a little over an hour after setting out on the great bear hunt. Using the main boom and hydraulics to lift the bears from the skiff, dip them in clear water and broom off the mud before depositing them on the deck of the boat was effortless. Gutting after careful skinning took about two hours with the three of us working. We hung the carcasses on the main boom, had a nice hot meal from the boat's supplies, and slept peacefully.

We offered the bear meat to the villagers, but since the smelly bears had been feeding on salmon, the local folks politely turned down our offer. I kept two hinds to freeze and take home for roasts. They did not smell or taste at all bad to me. Arne said they would find someone to take the rest of the meat, or, I silently suspected, he might use it for crab bait.

Already enamored with Alaska, this unplanned little hunt further solidified my love of the Great Land.

These were not large bears, so after having them tanned, and having a difficult hassle with the local tanning fellow who tried to substitute some badly cut and rubbed skins for mine, I gave them to "Gram" - my Grandma Nason, who made a queen sized bed spread from the three hides. She loved to show her warm cover to her friends in Oracle, Arizona.

I kept the front leg skins from one bear and later asked an Indian lady, Ruth Koktelash from Nondalton to make a pair of mittens for myself.

Once unloaded at the village, we had the field clinic assembled in about an hour, cleaned the boatmen's teeth, placed a couple of silver amalgam restorations, and our debt was paid.

1968: A Black Bear Encounter While Carrying Fish

In late August of 1968, after fourteen wonderful months in Alaska, I had a weekend free before starting my autumn village trips, so I thought it would be a good idea to catch some silver salmon to freeze for winter meals. I had a .357 magnum, double action pistol with a six inch barrel, which I usually kept in the cab of the truck for personal safety, but I carried it as bear protection when fishing, as well. I was still new to Alaska, and generally inexperienced with bears.

This particular Saturday I'd risen about four o'clock in the morning and drove my pick up with the plywood camper I built while in dental school from Anchorage down toward Seward.

A moderate hike off the highway took me to some holes that were loaded with fresh sea run silvers and I had my limit of three bright salmon in less than an hour. I was pleased to see no other fishermen in the area. But fresh bear tracks, made by both black and brown bears were plentiful. I hadn't seen a bear that morning, but the dozens of stripped fish carcasses littering the river banks and trails clearly indicated recent bear and bird activity.

The odors along this stretch of river reminded me of old, over filled outhouses that were in common use during in my childhood - repellent to the human senses, but apparently an irresistible attraction to bruins and birds.

I had the twenty pounds or so of beheaded and gutted salmon in a plastic bag inside my backpack. The hike back was easy, but, as the last half-mile or so of the trail was through dense brush and long grass, I was a bit anxious, after seeing all the fresh bear sign. I had the pistol in a holster inside my jacket, ready to deploy, should the need arise.

The thought of a fresh cup of coffee and a snack in the camper was appealing to me, so I was hustling right along.

Both Brown and Black bears had been fishing "my" hole.

As I rounded a corner in the muddy trail, a slight breeze blew directly into my face. I saw what appeared to be a large Black bear about forty yards in front of me, walking down the trail my way. The bear stopped, briefly, I drew my pistol, pulled back the hammer and yelled "Hey !" I really didn't want to shoot the animal. My reaction seemed to motivate the bear, which suddenly jerked its head up to stare at me, then lowered its head slightly and came toward me - not running, but determined as it looked at me and came my way. At twenty-five or thirty yards I held for the bear's head and squeezed. The bullet struck the bear just below the chin and a little right of center, hitting it between it's left shoulder and its neck. I noticed a flinch, but the bear only twitched and kept coming, so I squeezed two more shots off, both of which had no apparent effect on the beast. I thought I might have missed. My fourth shot was at less than twelve yards, which caused the bear to make a hard right turn. I shot again at the base of the tail. The bear bawled and disappeared into the brush.

Well, I was really pumped up and shaking. I backed up, fumbled more cartridges from my right front pants pocket and replaced the five spent shells with live ones, refilling the cylinder. I now again had six rounds in the pistol and one left in my pocket. I felt twitchy, but better.

1968: A Black Bear Encounter While Carrying Fish

I heard the brush crack from where the bear had entered, but I did not advance. The silence was a bit unnerving. I stood absolutely still, listening. I could clearly hear my heart beating - that, and a magpie was all.

I forced myself to wait a full five minutes by my wrist watch, then, ever so carefully, I approached the place I'd last seen the bear. I was on full alert and really twitchy. My pistol was ready -" hot" with the hammer back and cocked.

A broken alder indicated the spot the bear departed the trail and it's leaves about two feet off the ground showed plenty of bright red blood. I peered into the brush. There lay the bear! It was just a black shadow about five yards into the thicket. I saw no indication of life or breathing by the bear, but I was breathing rapidly and noisily. With the pistol aimed at it, I watched that black hair ball for two or three minutes, then retrieved my fishing pole and used it to poke the carcass. There was no motion. I stood back, nervously watching the black hair ball.

I was expecting someone to come along the trail, but no one showed up. After another wait of several minutes duration, I poked the bear again. There was no reaction. I squeezed through the brush to look at the head. The eyes were open and did not react to me poking them with the pole, so I grabbed a hind foot with my left hand and gave it a pull. It was just dead weight. I jerked it along repeatedly to bring it out of the dense underbrush. Then I holstered the pistol and drug the carcass to some grass alongside the trail. As I did this, I kept looking around, hoping to not be surprised by another bear, especially one of the big brownies that had recently left their tracks on the trail.

Well, I estimated that blackie to be only about 150 pounds or so - about my own weight - with a beautiful sleek black hide showing a patch of white on the chest at the base of the throat. It had undergone considerable ground shrink since I saw it on the trail.

Man ! What a morning - and it wasn't even noon yet!

I debated going back to the truck with the fish and having a bite to eat, but decided that to do that and then return would be more risky than to just skin the bear on the spot and take it back with the fish.

My skinning was hasty. I left a lot of fat and some meat attached to the hide, but I figured the sooner I could get out of there, the better. I left the head and paws in the skin for removal later in a more comfortable setting. This bruin smelled almost as bad as the remains of the fish carcasses along the creek. So did my hands.

In my excitement I completely forgot to snap any photographs.

About 1:30 pm I got back to the truck, put the fish in my ice box and decided not to return for the hind quarters of the bear. It was far too smelly.

After a cup of coffee and a quick bite to eat. I was on the road back to Anchorage by about 3:00 pm, enjoying another coffee and sandwich on the road.

The first couple of bites of my second sandwich tasted like rotten fish. So, I stopped at the first creek and washed my hands repeatedly. This was not the first bear I had taken, but it was far and away the smelliest.

My first shot had not hit a bone, the second two were into the chest cavity and my last shot damaged the right ham. Each had resulted in massive blood loss.

Since I was renting a daylight basement apartment in Anchorage, I decided it best to flesh the fishy bear hide outside, rather than risk complaints from my landlord. I delivered that hide to the tannery on Monday. As it was early autumn, the bear was not well furred, so after tanning I gave it to a native lady to use for trimmings on fur pieces she sewed.

Well, I had been thoroughly shaken and stirred that fine day and I decided to look for a bigger pistol.

In Pursuit of the Ice Bear

Reading about hunting polar bears in the 1960s I learned that was among the most expensive guided hunts in the world - costing an average of one thousand dollars for the hunt in Alaska.

When I arrived in the Great Land in 1967, as a non-resident I paid twenty bucks for a year-long hunting and fishing license. I bought a deer tag, then a black bear tag for ten dollars each, and I paid five bucks for my first Assistant Guide license. A polar bear tag cost a whopping one hundred and fifty dollars.

When I learned that most polar bear hunts were conducted by two guides working together, each with a small aircraft and one "client". I was disgusted at what sounded like an unsportsmanlike manner of the hunting. One aircraft would fly out at a level of three hundred feet or so above the ice, looking for tracks of a large, single bear. Once a trail was identified as fresh, the pilot/guide would keep on it until the bear was located or the tracks ended in an open lead or polynya. A "lead" is a stretch of open water in the ice pack. Leads are subject to significant changes as the currents move the ice. A polynya is an area of open water surrounded by ice. Seals often are found in such areas and polar bears hunt seals.

Once a suitable bear - meaning single and large enough - was located one plane would land on a flat pan of ice. The guide and guest hunter would set up, concealed in the broken ice of a pressure ridge near a pan of flat ice while the second aircraft would gently haze the bear toward the waiting men, by flying low level, lazy circles in an area they intended the bear to avoid.

When the bear came within range the hunter would shoot and usually that was that. The second plane would land, photographs were made, the bear was skinned, and off the two planes went in search of another bear.

Often the pair of airborne guides returned to their base with a trophy bear for each "client."

Selectivity for large bears could not have been better.

One of the most respected polar bear guides, Ray McNutt, had tied his Super Cub tied close to my Cessna 180. He mentioned to me that he had not been able to find a fifty-five gallon drum in which to keep his fuel. He was a stranger to me, but when I understood his need, I loaned him a drum and a hand pump and I invited him to join our family for dinner where I picked his brain for information on hunting in general and particularly hunting ice bears. Soon thereafter, the partner of another polar bear guide had a problem with his aircraft and could not hunt. So that guide asked me if I would be interested in using my Cessna to carry a guest hunter and accompany him on some trips out on the ice pack. I eagerly accepted the invitation. I realized I could not have found a better mentor or a safer companion.

Once I, as a licensed Assistant Guide, had accompanied that guide on one trip, I saw the hunt from a different perspective. The remote sea ice, the often noisy moving pans of ice, the leads which opened and closed, and the harshness of the entire experience made me feel it was perhaps worth learning more about and investigating as a means of seasonal work.

On my first trip for an ice bear I felt similar to the way I had felt during my times on the ranch in Montana where we used draft horses for most of the haying and other work. We had horse-drawn wagons to go to and from the hayfields and to transport many heavy items from cattle feed to equipment. I knew when I first engaged in that work in 1958 that it was a way of life which would soon disappear. I dreaded its inevitable demise, but I wanted to absorb as much of it as possible.

On the Arctic ice pack, I had similar feelings. The public was clamoring for an end to this "unsportsmanlike hunting." Regardless of the healthy bear population and strict State regulation of the hunt, the "antis" were relentless in their effort to shut it down. This endeavor, this way of life, would not last long and I wanted to soak up as much of all its aspects as I could in the limited amount of time I might have to participate in it.

The Alaska Department of Fish and Game set the annual harvest at three hundred polar bears per year - which was believed to be a sustainable number. Though many were offended by the method of hunting, there was

A sow with a cub, a medium sized bear and a large boar.

no biological or game management reason to shut it down. The issue of different populations of polar bears and the many unknowns about their life cycle served to concern and confuse some people about the wisdom of allowing the hunt.

In the late 1960s and until the Marine Mammal Act closed polar bear hunting to all but costal dwelling Alaskan natives, Kotzebue was known as the "polar bear hunting capital of the world." Other northern villages popular with guides were Teller, Shishmaref, Point Hope, and Barrow. With the lengthening days of February, guides would begin to show up in Kotzebue. Most tied their planes down on the flat sea ice a few hundred yards from the beach. By mid-March it was common to see thirty or more small aircraft tied in front of town. Piper Super Cubs were the aircraft of choice, but I was able to make my Cessna work.

So, after just two seasons of helping with guided polar bear hunts on the ice pack, and several forays out to collect a bear for myself, the practice became illegal. I was thankful for my short time to engage in that interesting and sometimes downright exciting hunt.

But old ways die hard. Some folks, denied by law to hunt, wanted to engage in as much of the experience as possible. Many hunters truly do hunt for the experience, rather than just something to hang on the wall. So I took a few trips out on the ice to photograph polar bears in their natural setting. I always carried my rifle, in case one of that most aggressive species of bears made protection of my guest and myself necessary. But I never found it necessary to fire a shot while photographing polar bears.

On the chartered trips I did not use any camera as my guests were busy with their equipment and often needed my help. That was a mistake on my part, as those events, like so many, can never be repeated. So most of my polar bear photographs were incidental, like the one of the back bear in Montana.

Several years after the closure of polar bear hunting I took a French photographer all around in northwest Alaska one summer. He returned the following winter to film big game animals in the winter. I did get a few polar bear pictures for myself on that trip.

The remains of a lead, or perhaps it was a polynya, is shown on page 35 with four polar bears feeding on the carcass of a beluga.

With the onset of climate warming polar bears have had to contend with less ice and they are still struggling to adapt. From the mid-1980s to the mid-1990s approximately two thirds of polar bear dens were made on the sea ice, but by 2010, about sixty percent of the dens were on land, so I have read.

Three Bears Before Lunch

On a trip to Portland during the winter of 1976, I found a set of Edo 2000 floats, brand new and still unassembled in a crate. They were gathering dust in a warehouse near Vancouver, Washington. The owner wanted five thousand dollars for the floats which was about half the going price. I bought them on the spot and had them shipped to Kotzebue where we put them together and added storage hatches in the middle compartments. I put my second best super cub, N7156Z atop the new pontoons.

With this new means of access, we soon found virgin areas to enjoy in Northwest Alaska. I quickly realized that flying floats was really a lot of fun. I could take a much stronger direct cross wind on floats than on wheels, but taking off with heavy loads required more time and space. Rough water was to be avoided, but in most cases, a sufficiently smooth stretch of water could be located. On large lakes or the ocean, one had to sometimes land in the trough of the swells, then maneuver carefully to the beach.

With no rubber tires or shock absorbers, floats are the hardest form of undercarriage on the aircraft's frame and gear fittings, so one had better learn to land as gently as possible with a sea plane.

We could now get into some of the most beautiful country in the entire world during summer that previously, we had only been able to visit during winter by dog team, snow machine, or the ski plane. Often we had to be content to just fly over beautiful places, dreaming of how nice it would be to walk through the country beneath our wings when it was in the full bloom of the brief Arctic summertime.

The first summer I used the cub on floats at every opportunity, polishing my technique and exploring hitherto untouched places. Rivers with a swift current, especially when the current and wind were in conflict, were at first a challenge, but I learned to handle the situations as I encountered them.

My wife Mae loved the wilderness and we spent many weekends looking over new areas, sometimes we just beach combed and picked berries. Often we enjoyed an overnight tent camp in some of the most scenic spots imaginable.

Mae, for her Native allotment, was entitled to one hundred and sixty acres of land, if she could prove use. We had already built our first cabin at Trail Creek and thought a small camp in the Kobuk River drainage would be nice. On a flight near what was destined to later become the Sand Dunes National Monument, we found an "L" shaped lake that was perfect. No matter which direction the wind was coming from, we could land and take off from that lake with even a large float plane and a heavy load. It was purely duck soup for a Super Cub or a Cessna 180. And there was no sign of previous human use in the area.

The surrounding country was well wooded with black spruce and paper birch trees, cottonwood, willows, blue berry bushes, bog cranberries, crow berries, and other beautiful, tasty, and otherwise useful vegetation - like stinkweed for poultices. The colorful autumn leaves made it unforgettable. Mae wanted to claim forty acres here. So we set about getting a wooden tent frame for our canvass wall tent, a small wood stove, and other items ready to take to the lake. It was past the middle of September before we got back with the materials. We also packed some steaks, buttered garlic bread, corn on the cob and a bottle of red Mateus wine. We planned to kick this new area off with an appropriate first evening meal.

Of course we both had our rifles.

The evening of our arrival, black bears (*Ursus Americanus*) seemed to be everywhere. We counted more than twenty black bears within three miles of the lake. We set up the tent, enjoyed our grilled steaks, corn, and garlic bread, along with the wine and crawled into our double sized sleeping bag early, feeling very well fed and anticipating a great day to come.

We were serenaded by a pair of resident Arctic Loons, whose eerie calls added a special emphasis and an almost supernatural quality to the other night sounds. We heard the bass drum and symbol splashes of beavers that protested our invasion of their secret, private reserve as they slapped the water with their huge, flat tails. From off in the distance the lonely howls of wolves emphasized the ancient, pristine wildness of the place.

When dawn eventually arrived, which was becoming noticeably later each morning that time of year, we had a quick pastry, a cup of thermos bottle coffee and began to glass the nearby meadows. We saw a sow with two cubs, then a mature single black bear, which Mae said she would like to shoot.

After a short and careful walk during which we took full advantage of the ample cover, we eased to the edge of a copse of birch trees and began to visually search for the single black spot that would be the bear.

During daylight the black color, so outstanding in any terrain, is disadvantageous to the animal. I've often wondered why that color has dominated the species, especially in Alaska, where the lighter colored, or cinnamon, bears are rare.

Geese were calling as they flew overhead in large "V" formations.

Puddle ducks were vocalizing, some Pintails flew just a few feet over our heads. A pair of Green wing teal paddled around in the lake in front of us. A brace of Shovelers busily searched and filtered their findings for breakfast. We saw the upturned butts of three Mallards, with their curious little curlicue tail feathers as they dined in the shallows.

A Muskrat was making its way toward shore with an edible twig of something fresh and green in its mouth.

The aromatic wonder of the tundra's Hudson Bay Tea and other components of the botanical pantry refreshed our noses and reminded us of how important smells are to the hunter and the hunted as well as to the casual observer. I sensed the kaleidoscopic mixture of odors created by the land and plants as they changed to crisp autumn. And it was delightful. It's easy to fall in love with land like this, especially if you are sharing it with someone you love

With so many distractions I had to remind myself of our primary purpose that morning. I wished I had brought my movie camera to capture the wonder of all we were seeing. I resolved to bring cameras on every trip from that day forward.

Mae spotted it first. A small black smudge intermittently showed, then disappeared in the undergrowth beneath small stand of dwarf birch. She

Jake and a berry-filled black bear.

placed her upright finger to her lips indicating the need for absolute silence, then she pointed toward the area. I caught fleeting glimpses of what I supposed, and hoped, was the bear. But was it the single bear, or a sow with cubs? That question had to be decided before we could consider harvesting the animal. Straining our eyes, for a better view was of no help. The leaves were obscuring our line of sight. We had to move closer.

We each chambered a round. Mae, using a 30/30 lever action carbine turned her body to direct the sounds away from the bear and worked the action slowly, using her finger to dampen the metallic click of the shell casing's contact with the carbine's receiver.

The wind was still calm, but the sun was warming the air and the ground. The uneven heating would result in shifting air masses and eventually it would spawn light breezes. Soon light thermal currents would pass our scent in whatever direction the fickle zephyrs might drift. If the black bear caught our scent, it would run into heavy cover and be gone in less than a blink.

On shaky legs we crept toward the black thing's last location.

There it was! Seventy yards separated us from the feeding black bear which had departed the dense brush and was gleaning blue berries from the tundra as it slowly moved toward an open bog. It was a decent sized bear and it was alone.

Three Bears Before Lunch

Mae and her first Black Bear of the morning.

As it fed along, Mae took offhand aim and fired for the front shoulder. Upon impact, the bear sprinted forward, but stumbled and fell a few yards away. It did not show signs of life, so Mae reloaded her magazine as we paused to give the fallen black bear a minute or so, to move or not.

As we approached the downed bear, another single one showed up on the edge of a small lake about a half mile from us. We ascertained that the fallen bear was dead - its eyes frozen in a vacant stare. I tied my red bandana to the top of an adjacent bush and we went on for the second bear.

This stalk was less of a challenge than the first had been. We reached the line of trees marking one end of the lake shore and watched from behind a small stand of paper birch as the foraging omnivore worked its way along the edge of the lake. Back and forth from the water to the outer margin of gravel it moved. After some minutes, the bear seemed inclined to move further away from us, but at a hundred and fifty yards, it remained within easy rifle range.

Braced against a sturdy tree, I leveled my cross hairs on the bear's neck and squeezed. He dropped in his tracks.

We had two prime black bears after less than ninety minutes of hunting effort.

Curious about what the bear was finding along the shore and in the lake shallows, I found many large, soft shelled snails. These gastropods had thin shells with white interiors. I decided we should try some of this wild escargot when we got, or made, the time.

That beautiful September morn, we took 3 Black Bears before lunch.

Fleshed and ready to load into the floats.

The second bear was carefully skinned and the four quarters placed on my pack board before we returned to our first kill. A Grey Jay was squawking at the motionless carcass as we arrived. My red kerchief allowed us to avoid wasting any time or steps searching the still unfamiliar country for our prize. I pocketed my bandana and set about skinning the bruin. The carcass, wrapped in that heavy fur coat, was still warm, but rigor mortis had set in, causing us to take more care in making the initial cuts just right to "square" the hide. I added the four more quarters of meat to my pack and Mae carried the hide.

Both of the black bears were males, which I estimated to be of about six to eight years of age, and heavy with fat for the winter. Black bears, fattened by a diet rich in blue berries and other calorie rich food, make excellent table fare. Their meat is always tender, the flavor is mild - somewhat like beef, and when roasted, the drippings make the finest gravy. We brought all the usable meat out. Of course one must be aware of trichinosis in bears and cook the meat thoroughly.

On the way back to the tent, we saw another single bear, which was larger than the two we had already taken. We hung the meat and hides near the tent and struck out for the third bear. We were able to keep this bear in clear sight as we closed the distance, so the stalk was not at all difficult and Mae soon had that one on the ground, too. And we had enough weight for the cub to take back to town.

And it wasn't even noon yet!

We enjoyed a light lunch, then with a small fire - just for the primitive comfort of it, we began to flesh the bear skins in the pleasant autumn weather. We tossed chunks of bear fat into the fire and listened as they crackled and added to the heat from the wood. We could head back to town, but preferred to remain another night in our tent close to this pristine lake and go back the following afternoon. Our time in that relaxing, natural setting sure beat any time at home in company of the radio or television set.

We knew that this place was going to become one of our favorites. The lake had pike and grayling in it and at least two beaver houses. We saw one Muskrat. Deeply rutted caribou trails indicated their annual passage in large numbers. We saw a few moose in the area as well. Geese, several species of ducks, and loons all used the lake. We saw some recently made wolf tracks. Large fresh water snails were numerous all along the shallows of "our" lake and the adjacent ones. We debated tasting some wild escargot, but we never got around to doing that.

Beginning the next June, we made several trips each year to this lake, most times without taking any game. The beauty and solitude of the pristine country were enough to keep us coming back.

Mushrooms with markings of kaleidoscopic character grew in the goose poop and mud at lake's edge. I was sure they must be hallucinogenic, so for that and other reasons, - mainly my unfamiliarity with the fungi - I didn't try to eat any. I wish I had a photograph of those wondrous toad stools. We found small wild red raspberries which were tiny and sweet, but never abundant. They were delicious and really special. Cranberries, blue berries and crow berries were handy everywhere we walked from mid August until snow and ice covered the ground.

The loons. I think it was the loons that made our evenings at "our L" lake so memorable. Their calls were sometimes lunatic, other times pensive and forlorn, but always carrying a magical attraction. We began to refer to "L" lake as OLL for Our Loon Lake.

The aircraft pontoons, or floats, had enlarged our world, - already wonderful beyond adequate description. We were called to many beckoning, and as yet unknown paradises. It was clearly something beyond our imagination.

And we had only scratched the surface. We were stirred by the experiences.

Black Bear Uses

Black bears *(Ursus americanus)* are perhaps the most utilizable, and clearly the most frequently hunted and harvested of all bear species in North America.

In the 1960s, when I was guiding hunters for Black Bears in the Iliamna area, an older Indian woman and good friend, Ruth Koktelash, asked me to bring in the stomach of any bears we took in the fall season that seemed to be feeding on blue berries. Ruth asked me to tie off each end of the stomach with a small cord before cutting it loose from the esophagus and small intestine and removing it from the abdominal cavity, then deliver the berry filled pouch to her. She reminded me that if I had no string to tie the ends of the stomach, I could use a piece of tendon or a small strip of sinew from the top of the back strap. Nature often provides if one takes notice.

So the next time I had a guest hunter out that autumn I remembered to salvage the stomach for Ruth. I watched as she emptied the stomach contents into a large bowl. Ruth carefully sorted through the mulchy mess which in September is normally pure blue berries, many of which are intact, she removed the small bits of berry stems, leaves, and other small items. She did not rinse the remains, as that would remove the juices from the berries that had been chewed. Then she proceeded to turn the rest of the product into some tasty deserts.

This was much quicker and easier than hand picking the tasty little fruits. And only we would know how the berries came to wind up in her cobbler and pies. Ruth was quiet about it, but I was only too proud to tell how I came by so many delicious berries, at so little cost in time and effort. It was a somewhat pre-masticated bonus for harvesting a black bear.

Black Bear meat is also very fine eating in the Autumn, especially if the berry crop has been good - unless they've been gorging on fish or carrion. The flesh is always tender and the fat makes up into a wonderful gravy. I was surprised to find that bears don't have much of a back strap - nothing like that same cut on an ungulate. I normally took at least the two haunches back to camp for table fare, along with the stomach - for its special contents.

The hides are beautiful and vary in color from jet black to the creamy white of the Kermode (*Ursus Americanus kermodei*) bears found in a small area of islands along the British Columbia coast. Most Black Bears taken in Alaska are just plain, coal black, with some showing a small patch of white on their chest.

The "blue" or Glacier bear is a unique color phase which is rarely found, but occasionally occurs from McGrath to southeast Alaska. The glacial area around Yakutat is by far the most common place to find a "blue bear".

Cinnamon color phases are much less common in the far north than in the "south 48." In fifty years, after observing hundreds of Alaskan black bears, I have seen only one with auburn colored hair and one tan colored black bear. We were not able to harvest either one of those unusual critters due to their inaccessible location and other circumstances.

Most hunters have a taxidermist work the hide into a rug. I had a pair of heavy winter mittens made from the skin of a Black Bear that I had killed during my first year in the Great Land. They wore very well with smoked moose hide palms. They lasted for years, and they were warm.

All bears have a baculum, ospenis, or oosik - which by any of its names, is a bone in the shaft of the penis. This bone is dense and not at all cartilaginous, as one might anticipate. Some hunters cherish these "trophies" to use as stirring sticks for their drinks.

All bears, like many other animals including people, have gall bladders and these are highly prized in some oriental societies for their medicinal value. Since before coming to Alaska I had heard and read of people killing black bears just to get the gall bladders. If properly cared for, the contents of the bladder - the bile - fetched a premium price, if one could find a buyer. That practice seemed to me to be not only an illegal act in states that had made it so, but of much more significance, it was a serious crime against nature to kill such a magnificent animal only to use the contents of its gall

The lady hunter with a nice Black Bear taken above the Arctic Circle

bladder. I made it part of my routine to preserve the gall bladders and sold them until 1984 when the State of Alaska made trade in that commodity illegal. But my collection of the galls was only incidental to the harvesting of the bear. After 1984 I saved the galls and gave them without compensation to people I knew who appreciated them.

A couple of years after my wife Mae passed away in 1983, I took a lady hunter out in pursuit of caribou and black bear. She was recently divorced and mentioned that her ex-husband had never taken her on any hunting trips, so now, by Golly - and by divorce - she was spending some of her alimony winnings to plan and enjoy some hunts of her own.

It was late September and the Black Bears were out in force, while the mosquitos, white sox and no-see-ums were semi-retired for the season. The bears were stuffing themselves with blue berries and whatever other types of miniature wild fruits and most anything else they could find as they busily stored up fat for the long winter ahead. It didn't take long after one night in the tent to put this first-time bear huntress within less than a hundred yards of a good black bear, which was busily occupied with engorging itself with wild blue berries.

Inexperienced as she was, her first shot was true and after a short run, the bear dropped on the open tundra where it had been feeding.

ALASKA BEARS Stirred and Shaken

The lady nimrod modeling her black bear skin jacket and boots.

This novice Diana seemed surprised that she had actually killed a bear. Apparently her ex-husband had long wanted to do that, but after several unsuccessful attempts, he remained without a bruin in his trophy collection. His ex-wife commented that she found him to be just plain "unbearable" or some such thing. And now she had beat him to scoring on an *Ursus Americanus* !

She began to express her concerns regarding what to do with the skin. She did not care to have a rug hanging on her wall or lying on the floor, but as she stroked the beautiful skin she was impressed with the feel and warmth of the pelage.

So, I suggested that she might consider having a fur coat made from the hide. Bear fur is not as soft as plucked beaver, but it is durable and in this case, readily available. She was not a large woman and the bear was about six and a half feet squared. That single hide would be sufficient for a coat or jacket for her. In fact there was going to be enough yardage left over for a pair of nice boots, too. Each front leg skin would be enough for a boot for one of her shapely legs.

She laughed at the thought of a bear skin coat and boots, but after a little consideration she told me that she would see to having the work done. I had no doubt her one-of-a-kind outfit would draw admiring stares at any department store or ski slope she happened to frequent.

She donated the skull to a school science class and the meat to some local friends who were familiar with the delicious taste.

This lady went on to hunt other species of big game animals in Alaska. It seemed she had discovered a new and fascinating facet of life … as well as a source of unique and attractive clothing.

Fur coats have never been that appealing to me, but she looked really good in hers. I considered having one made for myself, but never did follow through with the plan.

So, the Black Bear can provide fascinating entertainment, exercise, medicine, the main dinner course, the desert, fine clothing, and a cocktail stirring stick as well, when put to its fullest and best use.

Spring Grizzly Hunt on Snowshoes

After helping numerous guest hunters take black, grizzly, brown, and polar bears over the past several years, in 1974 I had yet to collect a grizzly for myself and thought I ought to do so. I figured that it might sound odd to a potential hunting guest that I had never shot one myself, but more than that, I just wanted to do it and to have a nice big rug. With the recently enacted severe restrictions on polar bear hunting I feared that something similar might occur with grizzlies.

Same day airborne hunting of Dall rams, brown and grizzly bears was forbidden by law in the State of Alaska long before I arrived, which was a good thing in my view. One could not hunt these animals until after three o'clock in the morning of the day following a flight.

Since the Federal Government closed all hunting of polar bears by any but coastal dwelling Alaskan Natives in 1972, the Kotzebue area no longer had the winter and spring influx of up to eighteen pairs of polar bear guides. That translated to thirty-six airplanes tied on the ice in front of town. In good conditions, each aircraft would bring in a polar bear every day. Many of the guides often added grizzly, wolf and wolverine to their guests' bag, if weather and time permitted. The back country of Northwest Alaska had grown relatively quiet in the past couple of years, and the grizzlies had grown larger and more numerous.

The sooner the better has always been my mode of operation. And I was ideally positioned to pursue a big griz, having acquired a super cub in April of 1973. I waited for the spring season to open and sat comfortably at home, holding for a patch of good weather which was forecast to last for a few days. Barely into the spring season, the conditions looked right. One fine April morning in 1974, I gassed the plane, put some extra fuel in some of the old square five gallon cans, and took off to the north in search of a big grizzly.

The main problem would be due to the bears' habit of covering a fair amount of ground once they emerged from their den. Their foot pads often had a moss or fungus-like growth on them and on several occasions I had seen them lying, gnawing at the underside of their feet, shortly after emerging in the spring. I wondered if maybe walking about gave them some relief from itching or whatever, as they seemed to come out, walk around near the den, then go back inside. I figured I needed to locate a big bear that showed tracks leading to and from it's den, as often is seen after the first exit from their hibernating abode. They return and remain close by for a few days. If I found one of those far traveling bears, well away from their den site, having a chance to take it the following morning after spending a cold night would be unlikely, unless it had located something to feed upon.

I began my search in the Igichuk Hills just north and a bit west of Kotzebue, but found only two sets of sows with cubs and one small single bear. These bruins seemed to be ranging in search of something to eat, and not hanging close to anything that looked like a den nearby. Besides, all except the single bear were not legal and the single was too small for me.

Searching the willow patches near the rivers where moose were yarded up in large groups, I thought I might find where a big bear had killed a moose or found a winter kill and was still nearby. That makes for a considerably more dangerous stalk, but with good snow cover and no leaves left on the willows, a bear would be easy to spot. However after hours of careful searching, I found no such kill.

Late that afternoon I found one large single bear moving through open tundra, miles from any place that I could safely land the cub. I back tracked it for about three miles and found the tracks extended on further yet. Even if a good landing spot were available, this bear was cruising and would likely be miles away the next morning. I didn't care for the odds of being successful in trying to anticipate his route, land ahead, and ambush the critter, so I flew on to the north.

My search took me up several broad, snow filled valleys, but I found only three more sets of sows accompanied by cubs. I was looking for the old men's club, not the nursery. I was finding plenty of bears, but none were shootable, by my standards. Most were not even legal, as cubs and sows accompanied by cubs are not to be shot, in addition to being much too small.

Moose had long since vacated the head waters country in favor of the riparian areas further downstream and I was wondering if the grizzlies had done so, too. I debated on what kind of spot I might find to make camp for the night. I was sure I could find a willow patch with lots of snowshoe hares to shoot and take home to eat, and maybe I would have to be satisfied with that. I had my .22 rifle along.

Then as I crossed from the headwaters of one river to that of another late on that first day, I found what I was looking for. A large grizzly, which was no doubt a male, had made tracks around his den and it appeared that he had returned and was back in the den when I found it. I did not fly close to the den, hoping that the sound of my super cub would not cause him to come out and possibly vacate his den area. No bear appeared and no tracks led away.

Well into the mountains of the western Brooks Range, the snow was heavy and the temperatures were hanging around zero degrees fahrenheit at night. I landed a bit over two miles away, in a spot well out of sight of the den, where I made my overnight camp. There was no wind to advertise my presence to my intended quarry.

The weather was clear, windless, and cold with a full moon and I slept very well in my heavy down bag atop a dried Caribou skin mattress which I laid on the snow beneath the right wing. I woke up only once to look around my immediate vicinity, then slept until about six o'clock the next morning.

After some thermos coffee, a breakfast roll and instant oatmeal, I stuffed some dried pike, two sandwiches prepared at home, and some small candy bars in my pack sack, put on my snowshoes, and began slogging my way toward the den.

Traveling on snowshoes is hard work and with my limited experience in knee deep snow, it took me more than two hours to reach the knoll from which I could see the den site. I used a willow pole to serve as my third leg which kept me form falling many times. I was hoping the bear had not emerged and wandered off, but no sign in the deep snow suggested his departure. I unzipped and opened my parka as I tried to cool off.

Just as I was enjoying my first sandwich, in the "heat of the day", so to speak, the bear appeared. He looked around for a few minutes, then turned and went back into his hole in the snow bank. I continued with my lunch, wondering how long his nap might last. I was not keen on the idea of approaching the occupied den to try to draw him out, but I was giving it some serious thought, when twenty minutes later, he re-emerged. This time after a short pause in the sunshine, he began walking up the near side of the valley, coming my way. He entered a swale and was out of sight, so I shuffled closer to get to the top a small crest and suddenly, there he was, at eighty yards! He had covered a lot more distance than I expected in such a short time. When he saw me, he stopped, then began walking toward me. I supposed he was thinking he'd found a potential meal. Though he did not seem to be in a hurry, he was looking right at me and covering the distance much more easily and rapidly that I would be able to do in those snowshoes. With the Grizzly at less than sixty yards I held just below his chin and squeezed the trigger when he raised his head to look at me more closely. The 300 Winchester Magnum bullet smacked him in the throat and he dropped on his right side, stone dead, it seemed.

The shot made a loud cracking sound in the frigid air, with the echo repeating itself as it bounced off of the steep sides of the valley.

Immediately I jacked another round into the chamber and waited, but the bear did not twitch … not even a little.

I ate a mouthful of snow and enjoyed a piece of dried fish, giving the bear a chance to show any sign of life remaining in his large body. It gave me a chance to calm down and think things over, as well. It's a rare hunting trip that follows an intended script so well as this had, so I wanted to avoid any foolish action due to being overly confident.

After watching for 15 minutes the bear had not moved and careful scrutiny through my rifle scope convinced me that he was not breathing. Still, I used all due caution in approaching the beast from slightly uphill. I hollered, and when close enough, I pelted the motionless form with snow balls, but I saw absolutely no reaction from the bear. When I was close enough, I jabbed it in the butt with the muzzle of my rifle. I edged around to see that its eyes were open and fixed. It was deader than last month's news.

Spring Grizzly Hunt on Snowshoes

The big Grizzly was easy to spot in the heavy snow.

Skinned and ready to pack back to my camping spot.

I was elated. That bear would square over eight and a half feet - huge for an inland Grizzly - and it was a beauty! He had only one large scar on his muzzle and his hide was in perfect condition. The bear had retained an amazingly heavy fat layer after not eating for four or five months.

With the long spring daylight, I took my time, carefully skinning my prize, which reduced the weight I had to move the two miles to the plane. I left very little fat on the hide.

When I disarticulated the head at the foramen magnum I found that my shot had severed the spine in the upper cervical area. No wonder he never twitched! Literally, he never felt a thing or knew what hit him. It had been lights out, his switch had been just plain turned off. Game over for the Grizzly.

I began the return trip by dragging the hide to remove as much blood as possible before putting it on my army surplus pack board. The temperature had risen and the snow had softened remarkably. I began to sweat, so I took off my parka and tied it on top of the bear skin.

With the burden of the added weight, I floundered more often than I had coming up the valley. I fell down several times, so I went back to dragging the hide. The softened snow had become treacherous for walking. Staying in my own trail helped, yet even hustling as fast as I could, it still took over three hours to reach my aircraft camp.

I rolled up my caribou skin mattress, stuffed the bear hide in a large plastic bag, and packed the cub for take off, but the day had warmed up and the snow had softened a lot as the afternoon wore on. I had been breaking through with every step, making things dicey for the airplane, which had sunken over a foot into the deteriorating snow. I poured the contents of two five gallon cans of aviation fuel through a chamois filter into my wing tanks and stowed the empty cans as far aft in the cabin as I could. Each time I did anything to the aircraft, it settled further into the snow.

So I stomped out a short ramp to allow the skis to slide up out of the softening depressions in which they rested. Then I waited for things to cool off. Sometime after eight o'clock that evening, after a crust had formed on the top of the snow, I decided it was time to try to get out of there.

Even after adding the ten gallons, I was light on fuel which was a good thing. When I did make my take off run, the plane porpoised and broke through the crust at first, but as I eased off on the control stick pressure, the plane's gradual acceleration was enough to get the cub's big skis on top of the newly crusted surface and I was soon safely airborne. I believe that two hours earlier I might not have been able to get airborne.

With an overcast causing even more warming, I landed on the nearly snow-free ice in front of our house in Kotzebue and spent that night most appreciatively in my warm and comfortable bed after a hot shower and a toddy. I placed the hide in the basement, rather than in our meat cache, to keep it from freezing stiff.

In the morning as I was removing the paws and skull from the hide someone knocked on the door. There were two men in uniforms - a federal and a state game warden stopping by to visit. They did not know that I had taken a bear, but had decided to visit with me regarding what I might have seen of polar bears, as this was the second spring season since polar bear hunting had been closed to non-native individuals. So I poured them some fresh coffee to enjoy as I continued to work on the skin.

With a friend who also had a super cub I had made a couple of trips out on the ice to photograph polar bears and I told the officials what we had seen and done. I mentioned that I had observed numerous polar bear hides drying on racks in most of the coastal villages I had visited on dental trips.

With cups of coffee in hand, as they were checking and sealing my grizzly they said that they also had been to some of the villages and observed hides of sows and cubs on drying racks. They said they were shocked to see that females with cubs were being taken by villagers.

My reply was that natives hunted when, and made use of whatever opportunities presented, with bears being no exception to that generality. They had no reason not to take sows and cubs, as they had done so traditionally. Also, in that part of Alaska, polar bear meat, as well as grizzly meat was commonly eaten - even preferred - by some of the old timers.

Furthermore, when guiding for *Ursus maritimus* guides found most of their trophy-sized single bears closer to the Siberian shore while although the bears did not often den ashore, the Alaskan side had a predominance of sows with cubs.

The unelected federal bureaucrats that wrote the laws had practically no idea of the traditions and everyday realities of the people who would be affected by their rulings.

The bag limit under Alaska State management had for years been one polar bear per person. Sport hunters were limited to one bear every three years. Under federal management the limit was raised to three bears per person, per day, shortly after passage of the Marine Mammal Protection Act.

One man in a coastal village I served told me that he was taking twenty to thirty polar bears per year. The hair was used to make flys for fishermen.

The more distant government officials are from the public they "serve", the more absurd and counter productive are the rules they impose on everyone.

My Sister, Pat, Takes a Grizzly

During the late summer of 1977, my sister, Pat, came up from Kodiak for a month of summer in the Arctic. We'd enjoyed some superb fishing for Arctic Char. As matter of fact, most such Salmonids caught in northwest Alaska are Dolly Varden, but the difference between the two species is too obscure for most people to note and Arctic Char somehow sounds more appealing to many. We filled our creels with some of the other local fish including Shee Fish, Lake Trout, Chum Salmon and Northern Pike.

In early September I wanted to go up to the little twelve by twelve foot shack we'd built on our eighty acres at Trail Creek to make some minor improvements and scout the area prior to our guest hunters' arrival.

My sister, five years younger than me, and I had been hunting together since we were both in grade school. Our parents encouraged both of us to pursue our interests and our Dad often accompanied us on hunts, especially for bigger game.

Pat and I have been closer than most siblings.

We each went off in pursuit of higher education, and I to the service for three years, but in 1970 we again started to hunt and fish together when Pat came to teach school in Alaska.

We spent many hunting trips pursuing big game and Pat had scored on moose, caribou, a Dall ram and Sitka deer. But this trip was focused on tweaking the shack and looking the area over for our incoming guest hunters. Seasons and bag limits were very generous in those days and none of the big game animals in northwest Alaska required a drawn permit.

Since a Grizzly tried to join my wife and me in the little cabin back in 1975, we's had no bear damage, so preparing the place for the season took little time and effort.

However, our modest hut was surrounded by more bear tracks, scat and diggings than usual. It seemed the place was being visited regularly and often by a bruin with a possessive inclination.

During the first night, I was awakened by the sound of something rubbing against the door of the little hut. It was most likely a bear. I jacked a round into the chamber of my rifle and listened, but I heard no more sounds. Immediately my thoughts and concerns were for my super cub tied about three hundred yards away. I've seen some awful damage done to fabric covered aircraft by bears of all species, but I kept my flying machine clean of blood and I often scrubbed the floor and sides with chlorine solution to discourage bears from becoming too curious about what might lie within the plane.

It was a dark night, so not a good time to walk down to check on the super cub. Feeling reasonably comfortable that the aircraft would be okay, I was able to go back to sleep.

As usual, I was awake before sunup and when I opened the door I was treated to the sight of a hefty pile of steaming bear poop on the large flat rock I used for a boot sole scraper at the entrance. Nice! The uninvited guest left its calling card, along with some long guard hairs on the corners of the little plywood hut.

Rifle in hand, I peered around the cabin and into the willows, but saw nothing resembling a bear. The thing had come and gone by dark of night, but I suspected it may be lingering nearby. As daylight prevailed over the gloom of night, I walked to the airplane. The big tires and the gear strut step of the super cub showed some bear hair on them, so the night stalker had been there too, but it had only rubbed the cub, and done no damage.

Breakfast cooked on the Coleman two-burner stove was hot cakes and sausage, along with bread and jam.

By eleven that morning the sun was in full glory and ripe blue, cran, and crow berries beckoned, so we walked across the swamp and began to fill our buckets with the delicious wild fruits.

Along with the comforting solar radiation came squadrons of persistent, pestiferous mosquitos and white sox. We used Deep Wood Off as our sole counter measure but we might have been better served by a battery of heat seeking mini-missiles. No matter how fresh the application of OFF, some of the kamikaze-inclined bugs would penetrate our defenses and then our skin, raising itchy, sometimes bloody, welts on our hides - even on areas that we thought were covered by socks or sleeves. Pat and I began to take on the appearance of victims of a measles or small pox epidemic.

With our buckets full of fresh berries we made a hurried return to the hut for some lunch and to seek relief from the multitudes of tiny, six legged, flying, biting, arthropods that enveloped us.

I lit up two Buhach coils to rid ourselves of the insect hordes that had so smothered us they had become part of our silhouettes. The *Pyrethrin* component of the smoking repellent was not pleasant to our nostrils, but we happily tolerated the decidedly less than aromatic wifts which rose from the smoldering repellant.

Within ten or fifteen minutes the fumes from the burning Buhach filled the tiny hut and the mosquitos seemed to be beaten back, but some of the dogged white-sox continued their chewing until they completely penetrated our integumental protection, resulting in rivets of fresh blood. We resembled Indians decorated with war paint.

Over the past fifty years in Alaska, with as much time spent in the remote bush as possible, this was one of the most memorably miserable assaults on my person by the insect armies of darkness - and it happened right at home, in the bright light of day.

Pat and I slapped on some calamine lotion to reduce the itchiness, but I continued to scratch myself for the unique satisfaction it produces.

As the sun sank beneath the western ridges, things cooled off markedly, so we set out again to fill our berry buckets. This time, before our containers were half full we realized that we would soon have a visitor. As we picked berries, we each would look up to check the area close to us, then use our binoculars to survey the rest of the valley for game. This is a necessary precaution in Grizzly country, and I was thinking we should maybe take a fat bull caribou home if we found one within reasonable packing distance - meaning a mile or so. The nights had been cool enough to set the meat and it would keep fine for several days in these conditions, plus we had cheese cloth to protect it from flies.

But Pat spotted a medium sized Grizzly which was engaged, like us, in gathering berries as he swatted mosquitos, and he was on the same slope

The grizzly was coming for us. ULRICH HERBST FOTO

we occupied of the eastern foothills, about three quarters of a mile down the valley. Wind had been calm with only the infrequent zephyr from variable points of the compass. These were little thermal puffs, inconsistent and not dependable.

As the bear meandered its way north toward us, it would occasionally sit down, swing its head from side to side and lift its nose skyward, sniffing. Apparently the beast had picked up some hint of odor that had piqued its interest. As the distance narrowed from the bear to us, we both chambered a shell and left our rifles on safety.

Our berry production stalled when the bruin was within one hundred and fifty yards of us. After again sitting down, looking around and sticking its snoot in the air, the bear came suddenly up on all fours and began to rapidly walk our way. He had a fix on our location.

An opportunity was developing. I asked Pat if she would like to take that bear. She said she didn't feel like she really cared to shoot it, but if it was likely the one that had been frequenting the cabin, maybe she should dispatch the beast. The situation was as close to ideal as one should hope for. I told her to get ready to shoot the critter.

This member of the *Ursus horribilis* clan seemed bent on participating in magic - being transformed from a Grizzly Bear into a Parlor Bear.

My Sister, Pat, Takes a Grizzly

For sure this member of our neighborhood featured us as worthy targets, as it began to run our way when it was less than one hundred yards from us.

When the bear was about fifty yards downhill from us, Pat was lined up and steady in a prone position with her jacket as a rest when she fired.

The bear immediately twisted around and began to bite at its groin area. It had been struck by a bullet, but it thought some booger had a grip on it.

I told Pat to feed it another dose of lead. Her second shot as the bear was twisting and snapping its teeth, struck the animal high in the withers, a bit too high to do any significant damage, but the second hit and the roar of the rifle at such close range put the bear into a fast run toward the nearest cover, which was a thin collection of willows below us.

We rapidly made our way along the berry strewn side hill, keeping above the willow patch and watching for any sign of the bear. When we were directly above the highest point of the willows, the bear woofed and ran out the opposite side of the brush in a galloping rush for the safety of the thicker willows along East Bowl Creek.

Pat dropped to her knee and rolled the bear with her next shot. I thought the left shoulder had been hit, but before Pat could get another shot off, the bear had scrambled into the lace of riparian growth near the exit of a small creek that drained the foothills.

We loped along the side hill, watching the place we last saw the bear. The brush was sparse in this part of the drainage and the beast struggled out the opposite side of the creek and was soon into another, more dense string of willows which marked a small rivulet in a gully draining the precipitous slope.

This bear had been hit three times, but it was now in an ideal area to hole up. Daylight was fading, so I figured we should return to the cabin, then come back in the morning to dig out the seriously wounded bear. I hoped the bruin would have expired by the time we returned.

It's not desirable to leave a wounded animal overnight, but the thought of encountering an enraged Grizzly at close quarters on a steep, brush covered hillside in approaching darkness is even less attractive.

We walked, clearly dejected, back to the hut. A hot meal of beans, burger, and noodles, followed up by a fresh apple soon put us to sleep, after another thorough application of calamine lotion.

The night was cool at about twenty-eight degrees fahrenheit. A hot breakfast close to the Franklin stove put us in shape and frame of mind to go find the grizzly. A heavy frost still clung to the shady areas, but the newly released moisture somehow made the colors of everything more vivid.

The wonderful natural technicolor came through in the photographs we snapped that day.

I was reasonably confident that the bear would not have departed the last brushy gully. In fact I expected to find it stone dead, wadded up in the most tangled, obstructed part of that willow and alder jungle.

But, if by chance the beast was still alive, it would be prone to attack anything that came near - if able to do so.

The willows outlining the gully drew to a point at the top which was about fifty yards below some large rocks and an unscalable cliff. Narrow at the top end, the tangle was about one hundred and twenty yards wide at the base and from top to bottom the patch was about five hundred yards in length. There was a fair amount of square yardage for the bear to be holed up in.

Clearly the best way to look for the bear was to begin at the top and sashay my way back and forth down through the willows. My lateral excursions would be greater the further down the slope I worked. I expected - I wanted - to be above the bear when I found it. I left Pat near the top of the willows in order for her to be able to see both sides, in case the bear ran out. If she had a clear shot at the escaping bear, she should shoot it, but she was not to shoot if the bear was still in the brush, even if she thought it had a hold of me. People survive bear maulings more gracefully than they do being shot with a soft nosed bullet.

So, after placing Pat, I began to ease my way down through the brush. I was making plenty of noise without trying to be noisy - it was inevitable in a place like that. My noisy progress could allow the bear to figure some strategy to try to nail me, his antagonist, but that's the way the cards fell.

I went slowly, paying special attention to not passing anything that might conceal the bear and avoiding allowing such spots to be higher than myself on that steep slope. I would assure myself that nothing was hiding on one level, then I'd work diagonally down hill, then back and forth at the next level, and so on down the hill.

Pat with her boar Grizzly.

After about an hour and a half of slowly searching I smelled something. I'd smelled plenty of bears before, but this was different. It was a nauseating odor, hard to identify, but strong. I kept on with my lateral creeping, wired for anything that might happen and still bothered by the horrible smell.

Then, about ten yards downhill directly bellow me and at the base of a large multi-trunked willow, I saw a brown form move. As the bear raised its head to look at me, I sighted down my barrel and shot it in the base of its neck. That put the critter's lights out permanently and most important, it ended its long suffering.

Pat hollered to see if I got the thing. I told her I had it, and to come on down.

When I got to the carcass, the odor was intense. The bear had vomited right there where it was lying. I'd never seen that before and have not since, thank God.!

When I looked over the carcass prior to skinning it, I found my shot at the base of the neck had severed the spinal column, Pat's third shot had broken the left humorous, Pat's second shot had cut a furrow through the hide just at the top of the withers, doing no real damage. Apparently her first shot which was taken as the bear came running directly at us, had somehow passed between the front legs, creased the brisket, entered the abdominal cavity, and as it exited, it had blown away one of the testicles. I've never been able to visualize the bear's body contortion that must have been in place to make that weird shot possible. That was the first shot with the bear focused on us and in full charge mode, not writhing or fighting a previous shot.

The anchoring shot had been the one that broke the humorous, otherwise, the wounded beast would have traveled much farther. I doubt we would have found the bear in that patch of willows, or perhaps we would have lost it forever.

I believe that grizzly was in terrible pain through the night, so much so that it had vomited. That made me feel absolutely awful and the memory haunted me for years - in fact, it still does.

I decided that if such agony on the part of the animals we pursued was to prove to be common, I would quit guiding, maybe even quit hunting. But in the more than forty years that have passed since that time, I have hunted bears every year and I've never again witnessed such a disturbing situation.

Suppressing my bad feelings about how that bear suffered by making only a perfunctory comment on the issue to my sister, we snapped a few photographs which showed brilliantly contrasting colors when the prints came back from the developer.

We spent nearly two hours skinning the bruin to avoid a repeat of close fleshing when at the cabin. We did not salvage any of the meat of this bear, due to the odor of vomit. I still harbored hopes of finding a fat bull caribou to send to Kodiak with Pat.

We returned to the shack by mid-afternoon and pecked around with minor chores as we took turns glassing the area from atop the building for caribou.

We had a light supper and crawled into our sleeping bags.

A short time after midnight I awoke with a deep pain in my lower back. The pain was profound and came in paroxysms, the frequency of which was increasing. I felt like I had been kicked in the groin. But the discomfort was somehow different. I suspected I was having a kidney stone attack. I'd never before had a stone, but kidney stones had tortured both sides of my family.

After enduring the pain for several hours, I got out of bed and went outside to throw up. Of course I was reminded of the bear's misery of the preceding night. Was this some sort of divine retribution?

Pat woke up at first light to find me outside, standing head down and nauseous. I told her what I believed was the cause of my severe pain and

My Sister, Pat, Takes a Grizzly

Me, goofing around, tongue out, with the finally dead grizzly.

that I planned to fly the cub to Kotzebue alone, as I feared that I might pass out from the ongoing agony. If I did lose consciousness in the pilot seat, she would be unable to do anything from the back seat and we would both likely be in a terrible wreck.

Bent over, I made my way to the aircraft with Pat assisting as best she could. I told her that I was sure I could make it to town and that I would get word to friends to come and pick her up as soon as possible. But, if she got a chance at a fat caribou, she should go ahead and take it, then have the meat close to the runway to load for town.

Clear conditions prevailed with twenty-six degrees and a light wind coming down the valley. As the engine warmed up I uttered a prayer that I could make the take-off, the ninety minute trip, and a safe landing in town. I prayed that the conditions in Kotzebue would be similar to those at Trail Creek. Then I steeled myself to the hour and a half flight ahead, taxied to the southern threshold, held the brakes as I brought the engine to full throttle, and took off. Holding the heel brakes seems to somewhat relieve the pain, but only temporarily. Once airborne I made a steep left turn and was on my way to relief.

I've always carried a quart of water to sip on during flights, but I feared putting much in my stomach that would soon come up as vomit, so I minimized my intake to mere wetting doses of the fine Trail Creek branch water.

Heading south I cut as many corners on the route as possible, but the ninety minutes seemed to take half of forever. When I neared the mouth of the Noatak River, I called in to the flight service station stating my intention to land "straight in on runway one-seven". And I asked the man on duty to call my wife and ask her to meet me at the field. No other traffic was in the zone, so I landed without incident and taxied to my tie-downs.

My wife, Mae, arrived as I tied the final rope securing the plane, and she asked what was wrong. I put my rifle and bag in the truck and told her to take me to the hospital because I thought I had a kidney stone.

The old Indian Health Service hospital had a small waiting room, with only three people were sitting there - I still remember the faces of them all. I walked past the room and directly down the hall to the emergency room. A nurse asked me what was wrong and I told her I needed a doctor, but first I needed some morphine as I was in terrible pain.

The young physician that rushed in was recently transferred to that hospital and he was not long out of medical school. He showed a measured calm and was very attentive. He said he knew who I was, but then he proceeded to take a medical history on me. I told him that I wanted some morphine immediately and if he delayed it, I was going to tear the place apart. He seemed to take me at my word and gave me an injection of demerol that relieved my pain and made me drowsy. I was chagrined that I did not get to experience the wonders of morphine, but the relief trumped my disappointment.

X-rays did not reveal a large stone, but a tiny opacity near the urinary duct was apparently the cause of my grief.

The hospital did not deny care to non-native patients in cases like this, and the doctor said I would be given a room for observation for a day or two. I told him that I lived only a few blocks away and preferred to go home. I could return in a few minutes if necessary. So home I went.

Feeling sleepy, but not in pain, I called a friend at work and told my tale, asking that he go up to Trail Creek to retrieve my sister and the bear hide as soon as was practical for him. It was not an emergency. He went after work. Pat arrived that evening. She had not seen a caribou. I recovered overnight.

Huge Grizzly at Close Range

In 1978 I got a call from a fellow in the Seattle area who was a friend of a friend or had some such remote connection. The fellow's name was Bruce, he sounded like a reasonable man and I liked him right off the bat. Bruce wanted to hunt a Grizzly bear (*Ursus arctos*, formerly called *Ursus horribilis*) and he wanted to do it in the Arctic, as he had never before been that far north.

At the time we had only a twelve foot by twelve foot plywood cabin at the homestead camp on Trail Creek, but it was adequate for three or even four people in a squeeze, and it sure beat the heck out of any tent. A Franklin wood stove kept the interior comfortable and the solid walls provided a modicum of security from the sometimes aggressive bruins that frequent the area, as well as the omnipresent howling winds.

In those days, the cost of a fully guided Grizzly bear hunt was $2,500. Included were three meals per day, aircraft transportation from and return to Kotzebue with trophies, fleshing the hide and so forth. The guest hunter was responsible for buying his own hunting and fishing licensed and appropriate tags. The non-resident hunting & fishing license was ninety bucks, the grizzly tag was two hundred and fifty dollars and the caribou tag cost two hundred dollars.

There were no hidden extra charges on any of my hunts, ever.

In those days, when a new Ford pick up could be purchased for about four thousand dollars, twenty-five hundred bucks was a lot of money.

Hunting has never been cheap.

The entire summer we had been seeing a huge Grizzly around the cabin. That big bear would often sit on his rump and scratch his head, as if pondering a profound subject. At times he reminded me of Rodin's bronze sculpture called "the Thinker." I began to refer to him as "Old Deliberator."

I had been to within less than a hundred yards of that great beast several times. We had filmed him. He never seemed aggressive, which is usually the case with really big, old bears. However he was alert and quick to vacate the area if he sensed the presence of humans. But he often left his calling card - large paw prints and impressive piles of poop in the yard of the cabin. Judging from the gage of the droppings, one might suspect the critter that left them must have been the size of a horse. At my estimated eight and a half feet squared, this bear was about as big as Grizzlies get and I wanted to provide Bruce with the opportunity to take this outstanding bruin.

A friend of mine, Dwight, from Kotzebue had just purchased a Piper Super Cub and wanted to work toward getting his own Registered Guide license, so I signed him on as an Assistant Guide. However Dwight had no aircraft liability insurance, so I would not allow him to carry any passengers. Normally there is plenty of meat, hides, capes, trophies, and gear to fly back to town and having a freighter aircraft, along with Dwight's companionship, would be wonderful. I was flying commercially when not engaged in other pursuits and had plenty of insurance coverage for passengers, but the insurance applied to only my own aircraft with me as the pilot.

We flew the two cubs to Trail Creek and enjoyed steak and lobster tails (Dwight's favorite) for the first supper and hit the sacks with full bellies, along with hope and expectation for the coming days of wilderness hunting.

After a hearty breakfast we waded across the main river and climbed to a high knob to begin glassing the valley. A scattering of caribou were drifting peacefully down the valley as they grazed on lichens and briefly browsed the willows on their annual fall migration toward their wintering grounds to the south. It was a pastoral scene worthy of deep introspection and gratitude for life. As has long been my habit, I thanked God for our unsurpassed blessings, and we all agreed on how lucky we were to be Americans ... and to be sitting on the tundra in wild Alaska.

Within an hour we had made the first Grizzly sighting, but the large bruin was soon seen to be a sow accompanied by two small cubs. The bears held our attention for more than two hours as the sow slurped up blue berries and occasionally swatted a pestiferous cub. The cubs seemed totally preoccupied with harassing each other, but they obediently stayed close to their mamma. Their carefree frolics were far more entertaining than any scripted movie could have been.

The next day we glassed two individual bears, but I was convinced that not only were they not "Old Deliberator," but they were too small to spend much time investigating more closely. A good set of binoculars and a spotting scope saved us a lot of unnecessary foot work that day.

As we forded the main channel of Trail Creek some large Arctic Char (*Salvelinus alpinus*) splashed away from under our feet. Bruce was impressed when I explained that the big fish were a species of trout, rather than salmon. He expressed interest in catching and eating one, but I told him that they had come so far from salt water, their depleted fat and oils made them far from prime as table fare. Some fall spawning char have been in the river and not feeding for about a year. Furthermore, though we saw dozens of the fish, this was a major spawning stream and we seldom took any fish from it. If he wanted to taste good char, we would fly down to the mouth of the Kuguroruk River one day and catch some fresh sea-run fish.

The next morning I climbed on top of the cabin and glassed for about an hour, but found only Dall sheep (*Ovis dalli*) grazing peacefully on the mountains east and west of our shelter.

It seemed like a good day to go fishing.

We departed with both cubs and emergency gear and flew down Trail Creek, then followed the twists and turns of the Kuguroruk to its junction with the Noatak River. True to form, the big eddy just below the mouth of the "Koog" was full of fish. The finny beauties were stacked up like cord wood and seemed overcrowded and bored. We got a strike on every cast.

We kept only two six to eight pounders of the bright fresh-from-the-sea fish and planned to bake them over a fire in tinfoil for supper back at the little hunting shack.

As we flew back up toward the cabin I noticed something unusual just off the river.

I pulled back the throttle, dropped a notch of flaps, radioed Dwight, and circled back to inspect it. I observed a large area of willow brush that was all torn up. On a low level, slow fly-by with full flaps on, I was sure I detected a moose lower leg and hoof sticking out from one end of the pile of detritus. This was obviously a bear cache. Apparently a bear had killed a moose and after dining, covered up the site.

The position was as ideal as one could imagine. We could land on a nearby gravel bar, set up a tent, and then, the following morning cautiously approach the kill site which was near the edge of a steep cut bank. If the bear was not on the kill, we had a perfectly designed high point on which to conceal ourselves as we waited for the bear to return. The most likely route of the bruin's return would be over a flat, brush-free dry river channel which separated the cut bank from a stand of black spruce and cottonwoods which were rooted about one hundred eighty yards away from the kill site. The area I expected the bear to traverse was like a manicured golf course.

We returned to the cabin, gathered up a tent and other things to make the overnight camp more comfortable and returned to land on the gravel bar.

A fire to cook the char might alert the bear, so we placed the fish on dampened moss and left them by the river for cooking whenever conditions allowed. A cold supper was in order.

We had to wait until after three o'clock the following morning to shoot, so we decided to rise early and make our way very carefully as we approached the cache from the river side. The brush was dense around the pile of meat and could easily conceal the owner of the cache.

After a fitful night of lying on thin foam pads which inadequately cushioned our prone forms from the ubiquitous rocks, I awoke first and roused the others. We had only a fifteen minute walk to the kill site, so we took our time.

We would be at extremely close quarters in dense willow brush when we came to the kill site, so I put a shell up the spout, flipped the safety on, and told the others to do the same. Proceeding the last fifty yards with pauses after each step, we were all concentrating on whatever might come our way.

Usually a bear will give a woof or a throaty warning noise before either running away or coming forward. We were acutely tuned in and prepared for the sudden rush of an enraged bear. The day was warm and we wore only light jackets.

The cache had been visited since our fly-by the previous afternoon which was confirmed by the fact that I could no longer see the moose leg and

Bruce and me looking over the Grizzly's cache.

hoof. I reasoned that the bear had come back late in the afternoon or sometime that night and fed again, then covered up his meat bonanza and retired to the cool seclusion of the trees. Dominant bears scratch up whatever vegetation is available to cover their meat hordes. I believe this is done primarily to minimize transmission of smells which would attract other bears to the food source. Covering the meat also keeps it cooler than it would be if left exposed to sun and reduces access to blo-flys, however bears seem to not be bothered by putrid meat and maggots - in fact, I wonder if they do not prefer it a bit ripened by bacteria and spiced with juicy maggots.

We were ready for a long wait and had a thermos of coffee, sandwiches and cookies to enjoy as the time passed. With what appeared to be the large bore poop piles and some impressive paw prints of only one bear, I expected a long wait, perhaps until nearly dark, before the claimant of the cache returned to gorge again. I would have bet heavy money on this bear being an old boar.

Our best place to wait was only five yards from the hidden meat. It was not impossible that the bear might come back from a different direction - possibly from behind us, so I had Dwight keep an eye in that direction,

Bruce and me with the huge boar.

while Bruce and I kept close watch on the open field over which I expected the bear to come.

A few sea gulls flew by now and then throughout the day, and ravens "kauked" as they flew overhead, but none seemed interested in the bear cache. I thought that was unusual behavior as scavenger birds usually locate and feed off of such sites soon after they are formed. Often ravens, jays and magpies hop around nibbling bits of meat or fat while the bear is feeding. The bruin swats at the irritating birds which hop or fly away, then return to poach more tidbits. In the bears absences birds are capable of clearing away the coverage of the meat sufficiently for them to feed. Not even a gray jay had found the trove of still fresh meat. In fact, I noticed no bird droppings and not a single fly was trying to take advantage of the ample protein treasure.

Midday came and we each had a hearty sandwich. In the warm, windless conditions, I became sleepy, so I stretched out on the mattress of soft moss for a nap. Bruce said he was not in the mood to sleep. The moss and grass of the tundra made a much more comfortable bed than the rocks on the gravel bar of the night before. I dozed off into a deep sleep such that when I awoke, at first I did not know where I was.

Huge Grizzly at Close Range

A grizzly like that demands plenty admiration.

About three o'clock by my watch, which is actually solar midday in that latitude, I settled in at the edge of the cut bank next to Bruce. We had not seen a single big game animal so far that entire day.

Bruce asked when I thought the bear would come. I told him that would probably be about five o'clock - the normal time for dinner.

At twelve minutes before five, I heard the staccato chatter of a pine squirrel in the copse of black spruce timber across the open field. When I heard the squirrel scolding again, I nudged Bruce and tossed a stick toward Dwight.

Near the base of a large spruce tree I thought I detected a movement. I strained my eyes trying to discern a form, but I could not make out anything in the dark shadows.

Then, in that same place I saw something move again. After a few seconds, a huge bear slowly emerged from the timber. The animal stopped near the edge of the clearing and gazed to the right and left. Apparently satisfied, the great beast lumbered directly toward us, or rather, toward his private hoard of meat.

In a whisper, I told Bruce to take his safety off and get ready. I motioned for Dwight to come over and join us. I left my safety on. I was wishing I had my movie camera, but I'd had not brought it on this trip.

Without a pause, the grizzly walked straight to us. When he was directly below us and not more than thirty yards away I nodded to Bruce to shoot. The bear was offering a slight quartering shot and Bruce held for just behind the right ear. At the report of Bruce's .300 Winchester Magnum, the great bear fell forward on its nose. The factory 180 grain slug shattered the spinal column and the bear was dead before he hit the ground. Bruce jacked another round into his barrel and we watched for movement.

The bear never twitched.

We restrained ourselves for about five minutes. From our position I could see that both eyes were wide open, starkly staring into eternity.

In the photo on page 76, one can see that the huge bear's head is larger than my upper torso. The fur was thick and unblemished. It was clearly as good a grizzly as one ever sees. Though it was early in September, the bear was well furred with no sign of rubbing.

Things just could not have gone better for us.

We set about making photographs before skinning the giant bruin. There was no objectionable odor to this bear, so in spite of it having been feeding on meat, its flesh would be fine for human consumption. With such a short distance to pack, we took all four quarters to the camp site and when ready to depart, placed them and the hide in Dwight's super cub.

Bruce brought a good, but large, single lens reflex camera, so he is due credit and thanks for the photographs.

This was only day four of a ten day hunt, but Bruce decided he should head for home, as he had his bear and a heavy work load awaited him at

...nt, me and Bruce with the skin at my super cub.

his office. He was the owner of his company, but didn't get where he was by allowing fun and play to trump his business operation.

We flew up to the cabin, unloaded most of the camping gear and headed for Kotzebue.

The char would have to be cooked in the oven at home. Oh, well.

We landed in Kotzebue an hour after dark and soon were enjoying that one day-old char with a nice white wine.

After the required sixty day drying period, the skull of this bear measured close to twenty-six inches which placed him in the top fifty of the largest grizzly bears in the Boone and Crockett Club record book.

Judging from the wear on the teeth, I knew this was a very ancient bear.

The Alaska Department of Fish and Game biologist in Kotzebue, Dave "Sasqatch" Johnson, squared the bear at eight feet, eight inches. Routinely ADF&G removes a vestigial premolar tooth from each bear they seal. The tooth is sent off to a lab, sectioned, stained, and the age is determined by counting the growth rings. It is an accurate method. A year later we learned that this big bruin was thirty years of age, therefore born in 1948, when I was six years old. I've no doubt that this old fellow had sired many cubs. Over the next thirty years or so, we harvested more than a dozen bears in the vicinity that showed signs of being descendants of this bear. In 1984 we took a boar that squared eight feet, ten inches, though it was only twenty-two years old.

I joked with Bruce that it was a good thing that he did not hunt the bear while he was still a resident as it still had some growing to do. He had waited long enough for it to become a real record breaker.

Sometimes the stars and other things line up perfectly.

Grizzlies-Live Capture

Inland grizzlies are by nature far more aggressive than their larger cousins, the coastal brown bears. Sharing the same number of chromosomes, and often ranges, the two types of bears are capable of interbreeding and producing fertile offspring. I think the hard scrabble requirements of the grizzly's search for food at least partially explains their more aggressive nature. Brownies normally have abundant salmon to feed on for the majority of their nutrition, whereas grizzlies rely more on grasses, berries and whatever carrion they can locate or kills they can make. Both are classified as *Ursus arctos*, as are the European and Asian brown bears.

Grizzlies of North America are further sub-classified as *Ursus arctos horribilis*, for good reason.

The first scientifically reliable reports on these bears were submitted by Meriweather Lewis and John Clark, following their great Corps of Discovery exploration of the Louisiana Purchase from 1804-1806. They, and all the other men that participated in that greatest of all adventures, were impressed with the ferocity and stamina of those great bears. After several encounters with grizzlies, they wrote that they preferred to avoid them, whenever possible.

I've been blessed with many opportunities to interact with grizzlies, most of which resulted in the bear departing none the worse than before our encounter. Many of my contacts resulted in harvesting the bear, then seeing it magically turned into a parlor bear, after careful attention and wizardry by a taxidermist.

Working for the Alaska Department of Fish and Game for twelve years as a pilot and biologist, I flew my super cub in search of grizzly bears, then upon finding a candidate, I would call in a helicopter with a gunner using

Biologist Harry Reynolds and Jake pulling a tooth from a sedated Grizzly.

a sedative dart. Blood samples were taken, each bear was marked with a lip tattoo, a vestigial mandibular premolar tooth was extracted, some animals were fitted with a transmitting radio collar, and all soon walked away, unharmed. We never had a dangerous incident develop in these endeavors, due to the experienced professional biologists in charge. As I recall we caught two hundred and twelve grizzlies over the several years of the project.

As a practicing dentist I provided some extraction forceps and elevators to make the proper removal of teeth easier. Soon I ordered several dozens of the instruments, then sold them to ADF&G at the same price. Now, decades later, I see that those or similar instruments are still being used by ADF&G personnel.

John and Frank Craighead, well known for their pioneering live capture and other grizzly work in Yellowstone Park, accompanied the Alaskan biologists on two summer "catch and tag" projects in which I piloted my

A two or three old cub, killed and partially eaten by an adult bear.

super cub. I felt privileged to hear their stories in the tent camp, see those men in action, and to participate in the manner which I did.

The radio collared bears helped biologists learn about their movements, size of ranges, interactions with other bears, reproduction and survival of cubs, and much more about grizzlies in their natural state, as very few people visited the country in which the studies took place.

One female Grizzly I was involved with capturing, radio collaring, and tracking, had a home range of over four hundred miles in circumference. That is an exceptionally large chunk of territory for any land bear.

We learned that multiple sows with cubs often share relatively small domains with a degree of compatibility and tolerance, but I've seen dead cubs which were killed by other bears. Most often boars of the same species are the cub killers.

The coups de grace is often a bite between the eyes which enters the brain cavity. The bear on page 84 survived in good health for many years

An old sow bear injured by another bear.

after the injury. A German guest hunter of mine harvested the sow and we saw the terrible wound she had survived and lived with for several years. Reparative bone had filled in at the edges, but she was breathing through the hole between her eyes.

In 2001 while searching a large area of dense dwarf birch for a wounded wolf, we found a neck radio collar from a grizzly that I had helped capture and tag more than twenty years earlier. I turned the collar in to the Alaska Department of Fish and Game. That boar bear had been collared about fifty miles north of Trail Creek, where we found the collar. The collar showed slight damage from being chewed, but no sign of the bear that had been wearing it was found.

Grizzlies eons ago laid claim to the country within which sit my eighty acres, lodge and other buildings. Our little piece of heaven is one hundred and fifty-five GPS miles north of the Arctic Circle. I hold a Fee Simple Deed, but all the bears seem to believe that they are first mortgage holders, or rightful indigenous owners. Their tracks, ancient trails, and other signs indicate that they spend more time on the property than we humans do. Several areas show clear trails and foot marks that have taken decades, or perhaps centuries to form.

Grizzlies-Live Capture

Bear foot indentations surround the buildings.

Grizzly gnaw marks and rubbed hair on lodge.

We built the first little cabin during the summer of 1974. That hut, the first permanent human abode built in the valley of Trail Creek since time began, drew bears as surely as a pile of fresh meat draws flies. Within four years their deeply indented tracks were evident around the cabin, along with their shed guard hairs.

Every year we find their paw prints, gnaw marks, and droppings in the yard. Their hair on the buildings where they've rubbed give rise to my comments to hunters that it gets so cold up there that even the wood grows hair.

Bears gnaw the lodge exterior, but usually do little damage. Steel corners save the place from serious depredations by grizzlies.

Often, the bears are there, sharing the yard with us, too.

Always Best To Hunt With A Reliable Partner

We made a run with the *F/V REBEL* from Kodiak town to the south end of the island in early December of 1999. Our four guest hunters had paired up to hunt after hearing our stories about the high density of bears in the areas we planned to visit. In fact, we insisted that all of our guests hunt with at least one or two partners.

During a visit in his office, the local Alaska Department of Fish and Game biologist had asked me to take some blood samples from any deer we harvested that did not have two normal testes in the scrotum. He provided some test tubes and pipettes with which I could siphon off the clear serum after letting the blood sit at room temperature for a few hours. Once separated, the serum was transferred to small 1.2ml vials and kept frozen. The rest of the blood could be thrown away.

I planned to sample every deer I took - missing a full complement of testes or not - and as many of the other hunters' deer as possible. I instructed them on how to draw clean blood from the femoral artery of a freshly killed deer. It is a simple procedure. Blood from the chest cavity or abdomen is usually contaminated, so the femoral blood is preferred.

Tom Dooley and I often hunted by ourselves, as one of us needed to stay with the boat, but this day it seemed safe to anchor the *REBEL* and both go ashore to hunt, so we started out together. The wind was gusting to about thirty-five miles per hour in an offshore direction and snow squalls were intermittently reducing our visibility to less than one eighth of a mile. The weather conditions made it even more comfortable to have company in this bear dominated country.

We walked through the rolling hills that separated the beach from the higher mountains, noting a good amount of deer sign, but little else. As

A temporary bit of good visibility in the blowing snow squalls.

we approached a bluff overlooking a branch of the river, the visibility cleared enough for me to spot a large deer with remarkably non-typical antlers. I reckoned it to be a bilaterally cryptorchid buck.

Tom was about fifty yards to my right and had not seen the deer, so I shot it in the neck, knocking it off it's feet and over the edge. Tom and I got to the spot at the same time to see my deer lying at the end of its slide down the icy, snowy bluff. Days are short that time of year, so I told Tom to go on hunting. I planned to take the blood and other samples for the cryptorchid deer study, put the meat on my pack board and carry the load to the beach, then I would return for hopefully, another buck. We had only three days left to hunt, so no opportunities should be wasted.

Though we had not seen a bear so far that day, Tom told me he would eat his sandwich as I prepared the deer, then go on with his hunting while I packed the load of meat back to the beach. The wind was offshore, blowing up the bluff that the deer and I were on, and toward the beach. We had just come from downwind, so the likelihood of a bear being there was not high. But, we had extremely limited visibility, so Tom said he would stay until I was loaded and safely back up on the ridge. I felt bad

The non-typical, cryptorchid buck taken between snow squalls.

that he was sacrificing his hunting opportunity, but went about my chores. When I hustled, I could do it all and have the meat on the board in about twenty minutes. Tom said he timed me at seventeen minutes on at least one occasion.

When I had the samples prepared and was ready to tie the quarters on the pack board frame, I heard the first pistol shots, then I heard Tom yelling, "Get ready partner, I cain't (Tom's from Alabama, and he brought his accent with him to Kodiak, but never lost it.) hold 'em." Moments later two medium sized bears came off the bluff about twenty yards down from me, followed by two more and then a fifth, much larger bear. It was a sow with four big cubs - probably three year olds. I put a round in the chamber, grabbed my pack sack and scrambled up the slippery slope toward Tom's position, keeping an eye on the gang of bears as I went. I expected them to seize my deer guts, for starters, then maybe come for me. We knew this old, aggressive sow and her nasty brood from previous uncomfortable encounters. A pair of our guests had lost a deer to them earlier that season when the gang of five bears came in on them as they butchered a deer.

But instead, luckily for me and the bears, the leading two cubs continued across the river and immediately I could hear them scuffling around in the brush. Soon Tom and I heard the hysterical squealing of a deer.

Somehow the two big cubs had managed to catch a live deer and quickly silenced it. All five bears were then rousting about in the dense alder brush, tearing the deer apart, about sixty yards from my kill site. So I asked Tom to keep an eye on them as I took my rifle and pack board and went back down the hill to get my meat. I used double half hitches to quickly attach the quarters, carried the back straps over one arm and beat it back up to the ridge. I sacrificed the ribs - painful for me, as I really relish barbecued deer ribs - thinking the less time I spent in that vulnerable spot, the better. Clear of imminent danger, I secured the meat directly to the pack board and placed my pack sack over the load, ready to depart in a hurry, if necessary.

We wanted to avoid having to kill a bear and in this situation, killing one might lead to the necessity of shooting more members of that organized family group.

That evening on the boat, Tom told me that he was watching me prepare the deer when he heard a "wuff" and turned to see the first two bears approaching him from downwind. They were only about thirty yards away. He had a 9mm pistol which he drew and began firing into the ground in front of the bears, but they came on, oblivious to the gunfire. He pocketed the pistol and leveled his rifle at the closest bear, but they changed course a bit to their left, or they would have been coming down the slope in my tracks - and likely, without warning, been right on my back! Had Tom not insisted on waiting, those aggressive bears might have been on top of me before I was aware of their presence in time to defend myself. I'm sure that gang of ornery bruins would not have ignored me or been gentle with me, if they got close enough. I might have wound up as bear poop.

In a few minutes the sow followed by one cub, with fresh blood clearly marking their muzzles, came out of the alders, found my gut pile and rib cage, as they looked up at Tom and me, showing no fear. This old sow was overly aggressive and was training her cubs to be the same. Apples don't fall far from the tree and aggressive mother bears train their offspring to be the same, I have observed.

We retreated, keeping watch, should the sow decide to confront us again. But as far as we could see none of the bears came back up the ridge, so I continued on to the beach while Tom turned east to look for deer. I stashed my meat fifty yards of so from the rubber raft that would take one of us to the aluminum skiff we had anchored away from the beach to avoid being marooned by the receding tide, that's if the bears didn't damage it. Then I headed in Tom's general direction to hunt some more. We had more than two hours of daylight left.

Conditions were staying about the same. The intermittent snow and sleet squalls frequently caused me to pause until visibility improved. I was a bit twitchy after the initial bear incident and as I passed by a patch of alders, another, single bear of medium size rose up on its hind legs - not twenty five yards upwind from me, to check me out, then it turned and ran into the wind.

A big wind makes all critters, including people, more twitchy than usual and that certainly seemed to be the case that memorable day.

About a mile east of my kill site I saw a string of deer coming my way, walking crosswind. There were eighteen deer in all, with three mature bucks bringing up the rear. I hunkered down in the hummocks and waited until the does had passed, then shot the largest buck in the base of the head when he came by not forty yards from my position.

This was relatively open country with no brush or gullies to conceal a bear. As I approached my second buck, I saw Tom loom up out of the snowy obscurity on the skyline. When he got to me, I had the buck ready to load.

Tom said, "Well, Jake, you shot that one right out from under me." He had been following the string of deer, attempting to get within range for over a mile. I had no idea of his whereabouts. This time, the ribs came out, too!

That aggressive sow and her cubs were to plague us for the remainder of that season and the next. They ran three groups of hunters off of their kills and we always cautioned our guests that if they spotted a large sow with four big cubs, they should try to avoid them, in fact do not kill a deer within a mile of where they sighted the group of five bears.

I've only seen one other sow with more than three cubs, and I have never have encountered a more aggressive one. For a sow to birth that many cubs and keep them alive is far from common. She had to be an exceptionally good mother.

Sows raise their cubs to be successful, so I suppose an aggressive mother will promote that sort of behavior in their young.

So, once again the day's experiences with bears had me somewhat shaken and stirred.

Cold Steel by the Outhouse

In August, 2008 my grandson, Spencer, and I were helping four guest hunters in their pursuit of trophy animals. We had a couple of men from Texas, Chuck and Bill, a bowhunter from Washington named Dennis, and Chris, a naturalized Frenchman from Anchorage. Chris, though a Caucasian, had been born in Senegal, so he described himself as an African-American.

This was the last August booking period and Grizzly season does not open until September. We were sighting multiple bears daily. Most were singles, but a few sows with cubs were seen. I've not found a hunter yet who isn't fascinated by bears and other wild animals. Everyone loves to watch the powerful beasts from a safe distance.

We'd seen some interesting things. The first evening we watched a pair of golden eagles harass two adult Dall sheep in the high cliffs west of the lodge. I'd previously seen eagles knock a lamb off of precipices, then light near the young sheep and feed on it, but I had never before witnessed eagles harassing adult sheep.

The next morning we saw two grey wolves hunting the relatively open alluvial fan west of the lodge. The canines were working through the area, separated by fifty yards or so. They acted like retriever dogs searching for a wounded quail as they criss crossed the area with noses close to the ground.

Soon one of the wolves jumped a lone yearling caribou that had been concealed in a small swale. The chase was on. After about a hundred yards of running, the wolf grabbed a hind leg of the caribou and was joined by the second wolf. The caribou went down and never got up. Soon the wolves had removed a front leg and, as we glassed from the windows, one wolf carried the leg of the caribou south while the other wolf continued to tear at the carcass.

I believed the departing wolf was going to carry the leg to a den that has been in use for many ears and is located about four miles down the creek from the lodge. I anticipated the wolf would return soon for more meat and the two lobos would continue transporting meat to the den to feed a litter of pups.

I sent Spencer with Chris and Chuck down creek in hope of a shot at the returning wolf, while I took Bill and Dennis with his bow directly toward the kill. Maybe we would get an opportunity at either wolf from that position.

The wolf remained at the kill site for over thirty minutes, then, with a chunk of caribou meat in its mouth it came trotting our way. I had my video camera running. The wolf came to within fifty yards of our hiding place, then paused before slowly walking closer - to within thirty yards. It sensed something amiss, but stood broadside to us for several seconds. Dennis did not loose an arrow before the wolf turned back toward the kill site. Bill held his fire until the wolf was clearly out of range for Dennis, but Bill's shot at the trotting wolf at over one hundred yards was a miss.

We three walked to the kill and I recovered some fresh meat from the front shoulders for our table. I guess that's about like salvaging a road kill.

We saw a single wolf again that afternoon, but got no shots. On our return to the lodge we came upon a large bull muskox feeding on willows about a quarter of a mile from the lodge. As usual with muskox, it permitted us to approach closely, allowing some good photographs.

Spencer and I were each taking two hunters for the day, alternating guests and guides from one day to the next.

One afternoon we were glassing from a high point east of the lodge when a small Grizzly sow with two cubs appeared in the berry patch about two hundred yards below us. The three bears were enjoying the little ripe fruits, occasionally digging for succulent roots, and grazing on the green grass. They ambled, seemingly carefree, over the terrane, undisturbed. The cubs played as they fed. We had seen wolves several times in the past few days and as I watched the sow, she would stop, then nose an area thoroughly, look up and sniff the air. I figured she had smelled a wolf, or maybe us, and was somewhat concerned. Wolves can and do kill Grizzly cubs. On a couple of occasions I've found the remains of young bears that met such an end.

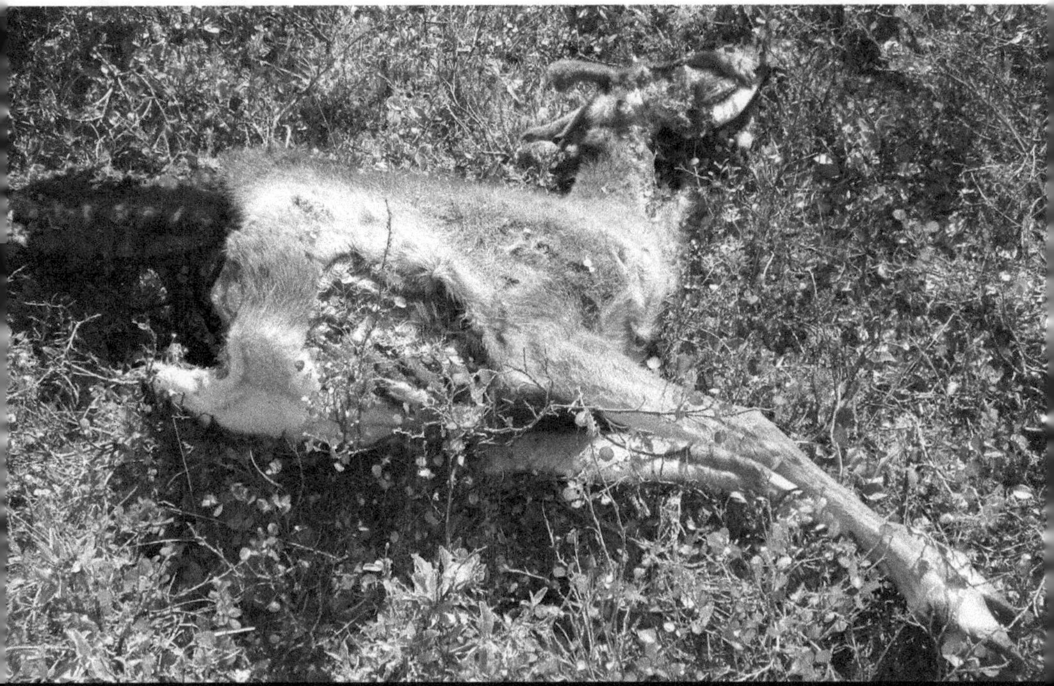

Cold Steel by the Outhouse

The two wolves took the best parts in a few minutes. Note: tongue eaten early.

A large, old bull muskox.

The three bears crossed the bog between us and the lodge and disappeared into the dense willows.

After two more hours passed, we had been hunting for the entire day and I suggested that I might head back to the lodge to get supper started for everyone. One of my companions, Chuck, a Texan, said he would like to go back early and take a short nap before eating, so I said, "Let's do it, then."

Leaving the other fellow at a good vantage point within sight of the lodge, we crossed the swamp and started down the trail to the main building.

As we came to the "far outhouse" (we have two one-holers) I noticed that a plastic bottle with a dash of creosote inside which I had hung by a wire, was lying on the ground. Furthermore, it had been bitten and torn open. I hang many such bear attractants around, as a means of alarm that bears had been by, and to hopefully keep the bears from tearing into other things around camp. Grizzly bears can't stand to leave something like that alone, they've just got to bite 'em.

I told Chuck, "A bear has been here since we passed this morning, it might have been that sow with her cubs. I'm going to put one up the spout" (chamber a round). He asked if he should do the same. I asked him not to do so. Normally there will be time enough to load and shoot if necessary, but I don't like having a "hot" gun in the hands of anyone walking behind me.

We proceeded slowly, watchfully. I heard a piece of lumber "clunk" by the sauna building and said loudly "Chuck, we've got a bear pretty close!"

At that moment a cub grizzly came running our way, but about fifteen yards off the trail. The cub passed and I heard the woof of an adult bear. A small sow was barreling right along after the cub. The willows were thick and she was on a course parallel to the foot trail. When she saw me, she turned, coming directly at us - and fast. She was less than twenty yards from me and had it not been for the willows which I thought might deflect the bullet to throw my shot off, I would have already killed her. Instead I waited, thinking I would try to brain shoot her as soon as she was clear of the brush. Just before clearing the obstructions, which would have put her less than ten yards from us, the cub bawled and I believe the sow became aware that there were two of us. She abruptly turned ninety degrees to her left and continued on her way, cracking limbs of the brush as she went. It all happened in mere seconds.

Chuck gasped, "Jesus, cold steel!"

"Heads up, it's not over!" I told him.

Another cub bawled from near the lodge and we could hear the sow coming back, again crashing through the willows, retracing her previous route. The cub was coming fast in its mother's footsteps and passed by, to be met by the sow, nearly in front of us. But to the benefit of men and bears, they were on the other side of the dense willow thicket.

Seeing that her second young one was okay, she turned around and together they vanished into the brush with the sow "wuffing" as she ran.

Probably not more than a minute and a half passed from the time I noticed the plastic jug, until the bears ran away.

We proceeded to the lodge, where from the top story window I saw the three bears working their way up the hillside to the east of the lodge, and away.

Chuck told me that he never expected to see such a sight. He said, "Jake, you were like cold steel."

I told him that during any close call, I get such a surge of adrenaline that I never feel a thing until some time later.

I also told him that we as well as the bears were blessedly lucky. It would have been a shame to make two little bums with no mother. There's no way they could make it on their own at such a young age.

A cold whiskey on the rocks, compliments of Chuck, tasted pretty good.

Spencer and the other three fellows had not seen our unanticipated rendezvous with the bears, but they certainly heard about it, several times, from Chuck, mostly.

After that incident, as time permitted, I began cutting willows between the lodge and the outhouses. Before I closed up the camp in late September, the area looked much different. Visibility was greatly improved. I have kept it cut back ever since, and I intend to continue to do so.

The path from the lodge to the outhouses is not like Hiroshima after the big one, but we definitely have better visibility during our walks to heed the call of nature.

Big Grizzly by Bow

In September, 1981, Bruce Moe, a good friend and repeat hunter of ours had been up to pursue a Barren Ground Caribou with his bow from our lodge on Trail Creek. Bruce had been here several times before and had always brought his good luck with him. In 1978 he had taken his first grizzly which was truly a monster in size. Bruce used his rifle for that hunt and the bear was an ancient genetic giant that placed him in the top 50 of the Boone and Crockett Club Record Book. In August, 1980 Bruce had taken an exceptional Dall Ram and returned in September after I contacted him with news of a super bull moose that had moved to within walking distance of the lodge. He wanted to take the moose with his bow and did so, as described in another story in a book yet to come, God willing. That great bull placed number one for the bow in the Safari Club International Record Book. My friend Bruce and I had been blessed with exceptionally good hunting ... and some good timing and luck.

Bruce was on a roll taking huge Arctic trophies by both rifle and bow, and next on his wish list was a caribou by bow. But he must have left his luck at home that trip, as during his stay we found plenty of caribou, but they were all traveling through open ground on the side hills, keeping well out of bow range. That's typical behavior for those animals, whose nature keeps them mostly in open country, from which they can run to escape most predators, but sometimes we can make an opportunity for a closer encounter as they cross from one side of the valley to the other, as the lay of the land forces them to pass through broken foothills and enter patches of willows and cottonwoods along the creeks. For twelve days we maneuvered, sometimes finding it necessary to run, to set up an ambush, but our efforts came to no avail.

When it came time to load up for the return to Kotzebue, Bruce handed me his bow, a Fred Bear Whitetail Hunter, and said it was mine to keep. He planned to buy a bigger bow and practice with it plenty before he returned for another caribou hunt in 1982. He also left his supply of a dozen arrows and kissed the bow good-bye, one last time.

My wife, Mae, and I had four days before our next hunter was due to arrive in Kotzebue. That guest was focused on caribou, moose, and also a wolf if an opportunity presented. He had no bear permit.

The day after I took Bruce to Kotzebue for his jet ride to Seattle, several bands of caribou had crossed the valley within a few hundred yards of the lodge. They were using the same route, which was well marked in the snow. It was an old route used annually by caribou. No doubt, old Murphy was grinning from ear to ear. It was such a shame that Bruce was not here for this scene and opportunity.

The following day one small band that had my attention was traveling downwind, as is common for caribou.

We saw the group of twenty or so *Rangier tarandus* as they emerged from the willow thickets on the down stream side of the runway, then we noticed the tops of more antlers, still in heavy willow cover, and coming from the same direction. I grabbed the bow and quiver of arrows, Mae brought her Winchester Model 70, in.270 caliber and we hurried to intercept the oncoming caribou.

Our timing was just right and within minutes of us reaching cover at the end of the runway, the lead cows appeared and walked past us - within forty feet. Tailing the group were two good bulls. When they were abreast of us, I drew back and let fly at the better of the two bulls which was not more than twenty yards from us. The bull stopped, looking right and left. The arrow had passed completely through the chest cavity. I readied another shaft, but after looking around, wondering perhaps what had bitten him, the bull stumbled and collapsed. The razor tipped arrow had augured a ten gage size hole through the chest cavity, and the animal bled out within a minute or so.

That was way too easy, I thought. With only two practice shots the day before, I had collected a bull worthy of the Pope and Young record book. I so wished that Bruce had been there to have an opportunity like that, but one has to take things as they come.

Timing is everything, they say.

With the hunter not due to arrive until Sunday, on Wednesday afternoon as a light snow fell, my wife, Mae was preparing some meat for dinner while I was reading a book. I had been getting up every few minutes to glass out the big window in the living room. I sat back down to read and Mae picked up the binoculars. She said she saw three very impressive bull Caribou coming down that same trail nearby which we'd taken the bull the day before. I stood up to set up the spotting scope and join her in watching the magnificent animals as they crossed the main channel of Trail Creek.

A slight breeze was coming down the valley. The caribou were walking downwind as they, unlike most prey species, commonly do. They paused to sniff what remained of the gut pile of my bull, then one threw his head up and all three trotted off, noses up and heads held high.

When they came to the main channel of the creek, they splashed straight through, without hesitation. Then they climbed up the stream's cut bank which was about three feet in height. They were shaking off on the far side when a huge buff colored grizzly rushed out of the willow thicket and knocked the lead bull to the ground. The other bulls trotted off about twenty yards and looked back at the grizzly, which made a short dash in their direction. That ran them out of sight. The bear's caribou never twitched after being knocked down. I think it's neck was broken by the powerful impact of the bear.

Mae and I were gasping at the sight and at our incredible luck to have both been watching when it happened. Timing is everything, or so I've heard.

This bear looked as big as any I had ever seen in the far north. Returning, it gripped the dead caribou in it's mouth, easily elevating the front half well off the ground. With the bull's hind legs dragging in the snow, the bear began carrying the carcass to the dense willows. The marks in the snow told the story clearly. Within a few minutes of the strike on the caribou, both it and the bear had disappeared into the thick brush.

Mae and I were still on our adrenaline highs.

Thinking over the situation, I believe the grizzly had winded the gut pile and was making its way toward it, following it's nose, when the three live caribou showed up.

Most of the bears we killed on Trail Creek were "known" to us in that we had seen them, sometimes for several years, before we found an opportunity to stalk them. This bear was a stranger to us.

Timing is truly everything.

Later that afternoon I went to the airplane to look it over. With bears always around I often check the machine for bruin damage whether I plan to fly it that day or not. When I opened the cowling and went about my routine inspection, I noticed a crack in the carburetor heat lever which appeared to be nearly ready to break off completely. It looked like it might not last for even one more pull, so I took a long, smooth rod from our oil stove, punched a hole through the firewall up near the rudder pedals and jury rigged the rod to function in applying carburetor heat on and off. It was awkward, but would suffice until I got to town. I called town on our single side band radio and told our daughter, Sandy, that I would be in the next day to get the broken part welded or brazed.

Thursday, as I departed I flew over the brush patch and saw the big grizzly lying on top of a pile of brush and debris, with which it had covered the fresh caribou carcass. I circled and flew over again, appraising the bear. It really was a huge one.

On the hour and a half trip to Kotzebue I began debating the idea of trying to stick that grizzly with an arrow. The positioning was handy, being so close to the lodge and all. I figured I could stalk pretty close without the bear seeing me before loosing the arrow and, with my Drilling (double barreled 12 gage shotgun with a 30:06 rifle barrel that a German guest had given to me) slung on my back, if necessary I figured I could use that to protect myself, if I had enough time.

The idea of arrowing the bear was intriguing to me. I was almost forty years old, but I was resisting growing up, as I had been doing for my whole life. It's more fun to remain a kid, I think.

I got the carburetor heat lever fixed and had a telephone message from the guest hunter, who said he would be arriving on the first jet the next morning. I decided to radio Mae with the change of plans and stay in town to pick the fellow up in the morning, then I could take him to camp a couple of days early. That would avoid an extra trip to town and save me over three hours of flight time in the cub and about twenty-five gallons of fuel.

As our guest hunter was not permitted for, or interested in a bear, I might attempt taking the beast with my bow, if conditions seemed right and the guest did not fuss at the idea.

We arrived at Trail Creek Friday afternoon, flying over the bear as we set up to land. The grizzly seemed to be clutching the debris pile with both front legs and studied the plane intently as we passed about three hundred feet overhead.

It takes a big bear about eight days to consume a whole Moose, leaving scats of diarrhea all over. The sudden change in diet from grass and berries to fresh meat does that to bears - and to people who suddenly change to a diet which is heavily laden with meat. I figured that a bear of that size could chew up a caribou in two or three days or less and Saturday would make the third full day the bear had to work on that pile of caribou meat. There was no time to waste.

Mae told me that she had heard wolves the night before and had seen three near the bear kill that afternoon before I returned with the guest hunter.

Friday night the wind had grown tired and was perfectly calm, but for the occasional light zephyr. We heard wolves howling and yapping from the area of the bear kill most of the night. I woke up several times to the noises. The racket was still going on after sunup.

It was apparent to me that the wolves had been harassing the bear all night and the grizz would no doubt be cranky, but probably sleepy, too. Mae was not in favor of my plan, but she insisted that she accompany me with her .270, if I was determined to do it. I thought that was a good idea.

Our Labrador, Max, sensed that something big was up and whined to go, but I thought he should not accompany us on this endeavor. The guest hunter also wanted to tag along, but I suggested that he post at the window and watch through the spotting scope, while making sure that the dog did not get out of the lodge until we appeared and waved our arms, indicating that we were finished, one way or another, with the bear effort.

Mae told me again that she was not keen on my idea. I assured her that I would quit the stalk if it seemed too gnarly, and that I would put the drilling to use, if necessary.

The weather had recently turned colder, but we'd had no big winds for some time, so the willows still retained a lot of their leaves, which made visibility a bit less than ideal, but the project was still doable, to my way of thinking. Such an opportunity might never come up again.

So, with the three barreled Drilling slung on my back, bow in hand, and Mae with her rifle, we cautiously walked down toward the bear. A slight breeze drifted down the valley, allowing a crosswind approach which was advantageous for us. As we neared the stream, I told Mae to put a round in the chamber and leave her rifle off safety - just in case.

If I hollered at all, she was to shoot the bear. I told her to expect the bear to make a kind of a hissing or woofing sound by exhausting its breath if he was going to rush us or run away. That's what I have often observed with bears on a kill or gut pile. Of course that typical behavior is not a rule, so far as the bears are concerned.

Bears have no rules.

We stayed out of sight in the willows on our side of the river, then crossed the creek at the same place the caribou had, our eyes always scrutinizing the brush, looking for brown hair against the snowy background. Each foot placement was contemplated and deliberate. No noise could be tolerated.

With us bent over, the cut bank gave us pretty fair cover. From the top of the cut bank to the outer edge of the dense brush was about thirty feet of sand and gravel upon which grew small clumps of brush. I planned to approach the main stand of willows slowly. Then if and when I saw the bear, I would draw back and let fly an arrow.

About half way to the edge of the willows I heard a branch move and before I could think, I was looking up the nose of an enraged grizzly at full charge, nostrils flared and showing the pink insides. I'll never forget the sight of the inside of his nose. It was pinkish.

He had not made any vocal sound.

So much for my previous experiences with the hissing bit.

Without thinking I drew back and released the arrow which connected with the bear just to the left of his head, burying all but a few inches of it's length. The bear veered and jerked to it's left, biting at the arrow. Blood spewed forth as if from a garden hose.

I knocked another arrow, but in my excited, spontaneous, and adrenalin-driven state, I overdrew, cutting my left thumb and forefinger with the side blades. With no specific target - just the brown mass of angry, writhing

Big Grizzly by Bow

Mae with P&Y Grizzly, 1981. Note blood on neck, the head of its caribou kill lies to the right of photo.

bear fur, - I let it go, hitting the bear in the lower back. The second shot was not a good one, but the first had severed the ascending aorta and coursed through to the right lung, resulting in massive hemorrhage.

Mae yelled, "throw that darned bow down ! " She was poised to shoot but held her fire as I was between her and the bear.

I dropped the bow and had the Drilling ready, but by then the big bear had gone still. He'd just plain leaked, or spewed out most of his vital juices, I guess.

Talk about an adrenaline high ! We were both soaring emotionally and remained so for quite some time. I reckon we were still twitching a bit, even an hour later.

Mae asked if I was sure the bear was dead. I confirmed that it was. She noticed my cut glove and blood dripping from my left hand. I had a couple pretty good cuts and I still bear the scars, but did I not feel any pain whatsoever at the time. I put some electrician's tape on the cuts to staunch my own blood flow.

We sat down in the snow and I told her that we had been really lucky … no, we'd been richly blessed and saved.

"Jake, I will never do that with you again," she blurted out. I assured her that I had no plans for a repeat performance.

My wife and I had clearly been shaken and stirred by the experience.

I reckon that the wolves, whose tracks were everywhere, had been heckling the bear for more than a day. The bear was extremely irritated at their attempts to get at his meat and was itching to catch one, but it appeared that under the circumstances, we would have served just fine as substitutes. Dominant bears take offense at anything that threatens their groceries. They are quite indiscriminating in that regard.

I was wearing insulated hip boots, size ten when I measured the distance from the bear to me when I let fly the first arrow. It was sixteen boot lengths, toe to heel. That's way to close!

Our greatest bit of luck came when the bear interrupted his fully committed charge to fight whatever had struck his neck. I've personally seen bears on a charge, after being shot multiple times in the chest, just keep on coming. Had this one done so, I would have been badly injured, or maybe worse. Maybe being hassled by more than one wolf had the bear thinking that he had been bitten by a canine assailant. Who knows?

We were lucky, no Blessed is the proper word. I do know that for sure.

It took more than half and hour for us to calm down. We got a few pictures, but our attention was not well focused on the job and the photos are not as good as such a situation and such a bear deserve. That's what a lingering distraction will do for you.

It might have been the intoxicating adrenalin high that fouled our photography.

We skinned the beast carefully. It was a boar. We intentionally left as much fat with the carcass as possible as we could take it to the lodge in the three-wheeler cart. Heavy fat would also make the final fleshing easier and the fat would burn hot in the sauna barrel stove. We had all day, so no hurry was necessary. Soon, Max escaped the lodge and joined us, adding his enthusiasm to that of our own. Max repeatedly jabbed the dead bear with his nose, showing us how tough and fearless a dog he was.

This bear was a sweet one. Prior to the caribou, it probably had been eating mostly grass and berries. It did not have any bad odors and we carried the two hams and the two front shoulders back to the lodge to eat and share with others when we got to town. As it is with all sweet bears, the meat was tender and the drippings made a wonderful gravy. The next day,

Big Grizzly by Bow

1981 P&Y Bear skull, hide, me, Max, Mae and ptarmigan with trapped red and Arctic fox skins hanging.

after the meal of bear roast, Mae put together a tasty grizzly stew. Had the situation been reversed, I'm sure the bear would not have prepared such an appealing meal … of me … or us.

That night the wolves tuned up again. For the next two days they yapped and howled as they devoured the remains of the bear carcass as well as what little was left of the Caribou. I think there were five to seven wolves in that pack. Though we tried to give our guest hunter a decent opportunity, he did not get a chance to shoot at any of that group of wolves though they hung around the lodge for several days.

The bear skin was sent off for tanning and it still graces our living room, draped over a rail.

After the mandatory sixty days, the skull was measured twenty-three and 12/16 inches and it placed number seven in the Pope and Young Record Book. By 1993 it had fallen to eighth place in that book. That measurement made it number two in the Safari Club International Book for archery grizzlies. Grizzly entries in either book are few, compared to the entries for rifle killed bears.

ALASKA BEARS   Stirred and Shaken

With Fred Bear in his Office, 1986

Making the book dominates some hunters dreams and efforts, but I have never been obsessed with placing animals in anyone's book. I enjoy the pursuit of game animals and never measure any the same day they are killed. I do hunt for the large critters of whatever species I am after, but I often take lesser animals, as my first concern is with securing table fare for my family.

However, the record keeping and book entries serve a useful purpose in that they provide a historical perspective of the size potential of each species and comparison of individual animals. The fact that records are being broken annually and that former high ranking trophies are displaced by newly taken critters that are larger gives us an appreciation of the effectiveness of big game management.

Although the caribou I took with the bow was large enough to exceed the minimum requirements, I never did enter it. I'm not a bow hunter, really.

Not being a practiced bow hunter, I felt clearly unqualified to enter the bear, but I was talked into doing it by friends.

As I was driving through Florida in 1986, I passed a billboard advertising the Fred Bear museum nearby, so I took the next exit and drove over to visit his collection.

After paying my small entry fee (two dollars as I recall), I left my Arctic Rivers Guide Service card at the desk. As I was admiring an unusual moose, with huge bases, but otherwise unattractive antlers which were still in the velvet, my name was announced on the intercom system. I responded and Fred Bear invited me into his office.

We shook hands and he mentioned that my Grizzly had bumped his from seventh to eighth place in the book.

I apologized, describing my initial reluctance to even enter it. He said that he was glad that I had put it in the book and we agreed that it is good to see that records are broken by bigger animals being taken in recent times. This indicates that our game management is working as it should.

Mr. Bear took me to lunch and we had a most enjoyable chat. He was a very humble man and I felt lucky and privileged to have spent that afternoon with him.

Timing is everything, I say.

Three Dutchmen Take Three Big Bears

During January and early February of 1998 I made what had evolved to become my annual trip to Europe in search of hunting guests. I spent most of my time in West Germany as so many hunters in that country yearned to visit Alaska which made my hunting for business in Deutschland the most productive use of my time in the Old World.

Seldom did I accept hunters from booking agents. Word of mouth seemed to provide me with the small number of hunters I wished to accommodate each year. Every year numerous agents from the United States and some other countries contacted me offering to provide "clients" but they demanded a commission which averaged twenty percent or more of the hunting fees, and I refused to pay such an extortionate slice of the total. However I made an exception in the case of an agent in Belgium, who not only accepted the ten percent I offered and represented no other guide in Alaska, but most important of all, this agent, Ludy (short for Ludmilla) and her husband seemed to be plain spoken and honest - with an accent. We discussed how the hunts were to be presented to the potential guests and I emphasized that no tricks, like offering free black bears in my lodge area, were to be employed to book hunters for me, as some agents had tried to do. I had not seen a black bear in the vicinity for about ten years. It seemed the huge increase in the grizzly population had wiped out the few *Ursus americanus* that previously had frequented Trail Creek. Guests were not apt to see black bears in my northern guiding area, and I wasn't going to have them baited with "free" black bears or any other phony stuff.

After making a Eurail Pass tour of German areas where previous guests hosted me and helped persuade new hunters to book with me, I went over to Belgium to visit with Ludy. She told me that we were invited to a luncheon the next day with a high volume fish wholesaler and a man involved with selling sperm from Holstein bulls. Well, what the heck I figured. There are lots of ways to make a living, but selling domestic animal sperm was a new wrinkle for me.

The lunch was delicious. Fish of several species and preparations was served, along with tiny wild bird eggs. The little eggs were blue speckled with black splotches and tasted about like any other egg to me. The host said they were lark eggs. I wondered how the wild stocks could stand this sort of pressure, but Europeans have been doing that for millennia and the wild birds in Europe seem to be in good numbers as far as I could determine.

The fish seller was a jovial fellow I'll call Lars and the wives of both men were very pleasant. The bull sperm fellow - I'll call him Pud, seemed a bit too self-important to me, but I've seen that often enough in people of all walks of life. If one is too selective in which guests he allows to book, he will be more poor than by being tolerant, and the first impression some folks give is not accurate. I hoped it would be that way with Pud. This looked like a good booking with three hunters and one wife as a non-hunting companion. That would fill one of my main booking periods nicely.

The booking/reservation was made for a period of fourteen days and confirmed with the guests payment of half the daily rate in cash. The Dutchmen were scheduled to arrive in Kotzebue on August 29, spend the night and go to the lodge the next morning by Cessna 206 charter. I emphasized that if they had extra time in Alaska, they should plan to spend it in Anchorage. They could maybe rent a car and visit Portage Glacier or other interesting places near the big city, or they could shop. I told them that too much extra time in Kotzebue would be disappointing, compared to what Anchorage had to offer.

Ludy was as pleased as me. I bought her a fine dinner that evening.

For the booking period preceding that of the Dutchmen I had a single hunter who was a computer programmer and was referred to me by a guide buddy in Arizona who said he was a good fellow, but new to hunting and had a tendency to drink too much.

That guest was very appreciative of the wilderness and courteous, in spite of a paucity of caribou. We saw plenty of Dall sheep, but could not pursue them because sheep were closed to sport hunting due to overkill by subsistence

Three Dutchmen Take Three Big Bears

users. The several dandy moose that paraded back and forth in front of us could not be hunted until September 1 or later. But stream fishing for the colorful Arctic Char and Grayling was excellent and the hunter finally got an opportunity to harvest a mature bull caribou. He was ecstatic about his trophy.

After dinner that evening I cut some wood for the sauna as my guest arranged his gear for the trip to Kotzebue in the morning.

When I returned to the lodge, the fellow was lit up pretty well from the remains of his special bottle of whiskey. But he was happy and effusive about his great adventure. I headed for my bunk, feeling confident that my guest would soon retire to his and sleep well.

An entertaining display of Aurora Borealis in the northern sky provided a great ending to our twelve days in the wilds.

Just after midnight I heard a loud crash in the kitchen and rose immediately to see what caused the disturbance.

The computer guy was lying on his back on the table with the window open and his head dangling outside in a drunken stupor. He had kicked over a pitcher of orange juice which woke me up when it splattered on the floor.

The poor fellow had the appearance of a bewildered zombie. He was disoriented and had no idea where he was or what was happening.

I was probably more shocked than disgusted. With utmost care to cause the least amount of damage to the kitchen area, as well as to the drunken fool, I eased him out of the window and off the table. I felt lucky that he had not managed to tumble out that second story window. I half carried, half dragged him over to the nearest couch and asked if he was going to be okay. He remained silent, but for some ominous rumblings coming from his gut. I could see that he was nauseous and soon to erupt, so I grabbed the garbage container for biodegradable stuff and got it in front of him just as he lost his booze-soaked cookies. I had to concentrate to not join him in his violent vomiting.

After upchucking all he had, followed by a session of the dry heaves, he lost consciousness. I listened carefully to his breathing which resembled normal, then I stretched myself out on the other couch nearby and was soon asleep.

My sleep was not sound. Twice I woke up and bent near the fellow's head to assure myself that his breathing was okay before going back to sleep. He was quite odiferous.

This ordinarily pleasant fellow really surprised me. His overindulgence with booze, followed by his self destructive and dangerous behavior were disgusting to me, but I reminded myself that we commonly see far more distasteful action from our politicians. At least this jerk's behavior affected primarily just himself while the misdeeds of our political hacks adversely affect millions of people.

As I was brewing a pot of starting fluid about seven that morning, the man woke up and seemed to be bright and fresh, except for his smell. He showed no sign of a hangover. He asked me how my evening had gone. I asked him if he remembered the events of the past few hours. He said he only remembered going to sleep and now waking up.

When I recounted the sordid events of the past evening, my guest apologized profusely and laid a hundred dollar bill on the table to pay for the broken orange juice pitcher and cleaning up of the mess. I thanked him and stuffed the bill in my pocket.

This guy was basically a decent human being, but he had a monstrous monkey on his back. I told him he really was very likable, except when inebriated. But drunk he was dangerous. I wished him well, and told him that the brightness of his future depended on getting control of his drinking.

He asked if I would ever go hunting with him again. I said of course I would, but I would ask him to stay away from booze on the next trip. I never saw the man again after he boarded the jet in Kotzebue.

After he cleaned himself up, liberally dowsing himself with cologne, and downed some coffee, he had no appetite, so we loaded the super cub and departed. Our ninety minute run to town was unremarkable.

My sister, Pat, had arrived from Kodiak that morning, so when I took the departing guest to the sod house to shower and change into his traveling clothes, Pat joined us to do some grocery shopping, and fill a bulk tank with aviation fuel while we waited for the evening jet.

As we slowly made our way to the fuel supplier we encountered the two Dutch couples walking along the main street of Kotzebue. I stopped the truck with gas trailer behind to greet the new guests.

Pud, the bull semen monger, lit into me with storm force. He demanded that their party be taken to the lodge immediately. He described Kotzebue

Three Dutchmen Take Three Big Bears

as more filthy and primitive than the worst village he had seen in Africa and they simply would not endure a night in such a slum.

Pud's rant was so out of place, I had to control my reaction, so I mentally detached myself from the vocal pelting he was delivering to me and waited until Pud slowed down in his diatribe.

"Welcome to Kotzebue," I said with a smile, as I held eye contact with this little wannabe bully. I thought I caught a glimpse of a smile flash over the faces of the fish dealer and his wife. The computer guy stared at the floor of the truck, while my sister turned her head away.

"Mr. Pud, your reservation does not commence until tomorrow and I clearly advised you to spend any extra time available to you in Anchorage, rather than Kotzebue, but now that you are here, I suggest you try to secure first class accommodations at the hotel, if they'll have you. After breakfast in the morning I will telephone you. We'll have to take your luggage to my house and sort through what is to go to the lodge and what is to remain here. Then, tomorrow afternoon, weather permitting, we will go to the lodge as scheduled. You might find something of interest in this Arctic community if you ask the desk clerk to recommend a taxi cab to tour you about today, but that is up to you.

The offensive little fellow's face took on the appearance of a piece of raw liver. I wondered if he might spring a leak or have an arterial blow out as he certainly seemed to have high blood pressure, along with a nasty, uncontrolled temper.

"NO, ve vill go to the lodge today -NOW, not tomorrow." he screeched.

"Quite not", I assured him. "I have a departing guest to see off, fresh groceries to purchase and other things to do in preparation for your two week stay in the wilderness, and the charter plane is not available until tomorrow afternoon, however you may pay the balance due on your daily rate later this evening if you leave a message for me and if I have time to collect it yet today." I handed him a business card.

"With that, Madames and Herren, I must bid you Au Revoir, as I am busy with scheduled projects." And we drove off, as Pud, standing on the side of the dirt road, continued to spew and sputter. I'd mixed my lingos in my stressed reply, but most Europeans are multi-lingual, and what can one expect from a resident of rural Alaska, anyway?

"Whew, that guy was really mad", the computer guy remarked.

"You should have jumped out and slugged the arrogant jerk," was my sister's thought.

We went about our chores, checked our man in at Alaska Airlines with his caribou antlers and gear, got things ready for the morning, and had a nice dinner of fresh caribou. It was no surprise that I did not get a call from Pud.

We rose early and had some coffee and breakfast rolls before I called the hotel. Pud did not take the call, but Lars came on the line, very respectful and pleasant. He said they had the money ready in cash for me and that they all would be pleased to see me whenever I could pick them up.

I told Lars that I would be over in precisely two hours to collect them and their luggage, and I asked that they have their clothes and gear to take to the lodge separate from that which they would leave in town.

When I met the party, they were standing at the desk with all their luggage littering the lobby. All but Pud were smiling broadly. They had a total of twelve large suitcases in addition to a hefty carry-on held by each. This was a pick-up truck full, then there was the four people to fit in as well. I stacked the luggage in the back, had the two women ride in the cab with me and suggested that the men hold on carefully as they would ride atop the suitcases, or they could call a cab, if they preferred. I tried to break it gently to the women that most of their luggage would have to be left in Kotzebue as the aircraft had weight and volume limits.

Once at the sod shack I invited everyone in. My old sod shack is substandard housing, but its a dry camp and has endured more than fifty years of abusive winter renters. My Dutch guests shuddered at the sight of the rude accommodations. I'm sure they were dreading the condition of the lodge.

Turning to Lars, I suggested that we proceed with their fifty percent final payment for the daily rate. As per our signed contract they could pay their trophy fees at the lodge when the hunt was completed.

The payment was made in U.S. dollars as our written contract specified. Pud had not yet said a word that day. Then I told them that each would be allowed approximately fifty pounds to take to the lodge. Pud and the two wives complained that they could not possibly survive for two weeks with only fifty pounds of luggage, so I suggested that they could pay for an additional charter if they insisted, but there was a risk that the excess stuff may not make it out at the end of the hunt if we had heavy snow. They decided to take the risk, so I called the charter company and arranged for an additional trip on that day and one more at the end of their booking. It was nine hundred dollars for each trip, I told Lars that the extra eighteen hundred dollars would have to be paid in cash that day. Without hesitation, he counted out the money.

So at mid-afternoon I sent Pat, Pud, and the wives with some of their gear up on the first charter. The Cessna 206 can make the trip in about an hour, while my cub requires ninety minutes. Pat knew where the key was to open the dead bolt on the lodge, the Honda three wheeler and trailer were out and ready and Pat could handle things until I got there. Pat held Registered Guide license #560 and had been helping me with hunters for over twenty-five years. I had no worries.

But Pat is not one to put up with abuse or arrogance from anyone and when I landed with Lars, after a delightful trip observing Dall sheep, moose, caribou, and three grizzly bears, Pat met us at the tie-downs and told me I'd better get up to the lodge as soon as I could. Pud was back in character again and it was not a pretty scene.

When I walked in Pud was in one of his characteristic rants and asked me immediately if the wine had been opened. I'd left a box of wine on the table which had been partially drained while the other hunter was in camp. Pud sipped at the wine in his glass, then walked to the sink and poured it down the drain, telling me that it was not the right temperature for white wine.

I told Pud that, yes, the wine had been tapped. He replied that wine should never be left open. I suggested that he observe the California boxed wine, which is all we used at the lodge to avoid hauling bottles in and out. Then I informed Pud that the wine belonged to me and that it was rude of him to help himself without being invited to do so. Furthermore, temperature control was not practical in that remote setting. I told him to not help himself to any more of my wine or other of my possessions unless I invited to do so.

Pud was not accustomed to being rebutted. I was ready to kick him in the butt when he asked me how many types of shrimp I had in my refrigerator. I pointed my finger at Pud, expecting that to infuriate him even more. As I shook my index finger in his face I told him that I had no refrigerator and no shrimp of any kind because I did not care for those filthy carrion eating insects from the bottom of the sea.

The incorrigible Pud drew himself up and told me that in his castle in Scotland, he kept at least a half dozen forms of shrimp for himself and his guests. I approached him close enough to bump him onto the couch with my belly and shook my finger at him again.

"Obviously, Sir, you should stay in your Scottish castle or any place that you can successfully intimidate and bully people, but that will not work in my lodge. Your early departure can be arranged at an additional fee if you desire, but unless you wish to be deported, you will conduct yourself in a manly, courteous way at all times henceforth, or I will eject you from my kingdom. I suggest that you do not tempt me further."

Lars arrived as I finished my spiel. I detected a faint smile crease his face, but he maintained silence.

I cautioned everyone to be very careful in using the rather steep stairs to the second floor, as a slip and fall would be painful. Then I suggested that our guests retire to their bedroom down below, as my sister and I had some preparation to do for dinner. I banished them all to the steerage section of the lodge.

I've never had to deal with a more puffed-up, obnoxious miscreant in my life. I was keeping my ire and temper in check, but I resolved to put up with no more of that person's vile behavior.

We had a nice dinner of pork loin, served with baked potatos, salad, a fresh carrot cake and the boxed white wine. Pud accepted a glass, then asked for another, which I formally poured for him. Apparently the wine had reached the proper temperature.

Lars dropped his reading glasses on the floor, then stepped on them, cracking both lenses. He asked if he could borrow mine, but I was using them and explained to him that I had only one pair, so "No" he could not use them.

My mind wandered and I began to wonder if I was being tested by the whole bizarre situation with these people. I reminded myself that I was responsible for everything here and I had to control my temper and keep a sharp eye on everything and everybody.

As we all began to drift toward our bunks, Pud's wife, Emma, smiled as she handed me a little book titled "Dealing With The Dutch" by Jacob Vossestein. She suggested I read it in order to try to understand Dutch people. The book had 108 pages, in small print, but I read it by Coleman lantern light that night.

In the morning Emma was the first to come for coffee and she asked if I had read the book. She was genuinely pleasant. I told her that I read every word and thanked her for the loan. Emma was charming, but I was in no mood to be charmed.

"Oh no, Jake, the book is my gift and yours to keep. What do you think of it?" she said.

"Mrs. Pud, that simple little book attempts to make excuses for arrogant, aristocratic, rude behavior. I, like most Americans will not tolerate that sort of conduct from anyone, perhaps least of all from aliens - foreigners. I expect - no I demand - that courtesy and respect be displayed by my staff and guests toward each other and I hope that is well understood by everyone." was my reply. "You would do well to remember that you all are guests in my lodge, my state, and my country and act appropriately. Your husband should understand that we own this place - he does not."

It was appropriate for me to mention that the book emphasized that the Dutch expected timeliness, following protocol and instructions, and being prepared, as well as following contracts to the letter. I mentioned that timeliness also applies to not arriving too early and following instruction includes not bringing too much unnecessary gear to a remote location - all of which was clearly stated in our contract.

Emma went back downstairs and I could hear her speaking with her husband, no doubt relating my comments.

It was not my intent to never again take a Dutch hunter - I had entertained some delightful Dutchmen in years past - but I hoped that I'd have no more like this bunch, and I was sure that they would bad mouth me to their friends. That was okay with me, as I wanted to deal with no one who was a buddy of the intolerant and intolerable Mr. Pud.

Pat began the breakfast which was bacon, eggs and oven toast, with canned peaches as a side. Everyone seemed to enjoy the meal and the conversation was centered on bears.

We had yet to sight in the rifles, so that occupied most of the morning. I was not impressed with the shooting ability of any of the three hunters. Lars' wife, Greta, the non-hunting companion, did not shoot.

I had expected the precise, deliberate shooting common among Germans and Austrians, but I was learning how very different these particular Dutchmen were from their neighbors.

The four Dutch, my sister and I walked to the nearby eastern moguls and glassed the valley as the women picked berries. The crop of Bog Blueberries (*Vaccinium uliginosum*), black Crowberries (*Empetrum nigrum*) and Cranberries (*Vaccinium oxycoccos*) was abundant and everyone, except Pud, commented on how delicious the little wild fruits tasted. Soapberries (*Sheperdia canadensis*) were so thick that some of the heavily laden branches touched the ground. Grizzlies feed voraciously on all types of berries, but they seem to prefer the red Soapberries, also know as Buffalo berries. The bruins meander through the bushes raking the berries off the bushes without having to stoop at all. But the Soapberries are well named as they leave a bitter, soapy taste on human palates. I have long suspected that the taste of those berries may play a part in forming the grizzlies nasty nature. *Ursus horribilis* may have its sour disposition due to those noxious fruits. Pud made a spontaneous negative comment on their taste, even after I warned everyone that they were not preferred human fodder. Oh well, I expected negativity from that misanthropic soul at his every opportunity.

Everyone observed Dall sheep, caribou, some moose and one grizzly bear as they occasionally sat to gaze through their binoculars.

We all enjoyed fresh blueberry pie that evening, following a tasty baked Chum salmon. Had Pud known of the five species of salmon and realized that we were serving something other than a King salmon, I'm sure he would have voiced his displeasure. But, contrary to his high opinion of himself, he really was not an authority on everything. The left over salmon we chopped into small pieces, added onion, dill pickles along with spices and made a spread with mayonnaise. It would make our sandwiches for the next day.

Lars asked for pancakes the next morning, so Pat cooked a huge pile of blueberry hot cakes. Greta asked that they again be allowed to pick berries and Lars said he, too, would like to collect more, so Pat took them to some nearby, but different hills. We all left the lodge about eleven that morning. I took Pud north. It was September first and grizzly season was open.

We walked slowly past Break Ankle Canyon, stopping frequently to scrutinize the valley with our binoculars. When we crossed Current Creek we proceeded up that canyon, following the "Bear Stairs", a series of paw prints impressed several inches into the tundra by millennia of grizzlies using the same route. The path led up the ridge bordering the gorge through which Current Creek departed the mountains. Near the top of the big alluvial fan at the mouth of the canyon we sat down to have a sandwich and glass the country.

Pud managed to utter a positive comment on the delicious sandwich.

Before we'd had time to swallow our sandwiches I spotted a large grizzly feeding through the riparian bushes on our side of the main river. It was browsing along, raking Soapberries as it worked its way through the brush.

Instead of continuing in the heavy cover, the bear turned and began walking straight across the large section of open tundra toward us, feeding as it came. It seemed to be headed for the "bear stairs".

Pud and I hustled down the bear stairs to position ourselves at their base which would put us within easy shooting range if the animal continued on its course. There was no wind.

This grizzly was a light brown, buff colored bear and as he swaggered through his grocery laden garden I figured him to be wearing a hide that would square close to eight feet. He was a dandy.

Between the open area and the narrow gorge was a dense willow and berry thicket. When the bear entered that tangle of vegetation we lost sight of him. He might turn down the creek or head back toward the main river, but I'd been in the same sort of situation before and I expected him to continue on to the much used "bear stairs."

After I had Pud stick a shell in his chamber and set the safety, I did the same. We froze in place. The tension was palpable and Pud began to show a high frequency shake as he stared holes into the willows below us. I placed my hand on his forearm and whispered to him that "all is okay, we must wait".

When I saw a branch move, I squeezed Pud's arm and indicated with my head where the bear was located.

For the next several minutes the bear showed briefly, then disappeared as it foraged. I could hear the bear make a splash as it came across the creek toward us. An open spot in the willows was just forty yards below and the bear stepped into it, still intent on stuffing its belly with berries.

Pud was aiming at the beast which would not be in clear sight much longer. I whispered - NOW. The blast of Pud's 8mm rifle was deafening.

The bear simply dropped to its belly and did not move from its position in the rocks on our side of the stream.

There had been no opportunity to coach Pud on where to aim, but his bullet struck the bear at the base of its neck on the left side and burrowed its way into the chest cavity, severing the ascending aorta and continuing through the right lung, before stopping at the skin in front of the right hind leg. Normally a shot like that would result in the bear tearing of on a full run, then dropping in fifty yards or so as it lost blood pressure. But this shot just plainly pole-axed the critter. It was a very old boar with teeth worn down to the gum line, but in robust physical condition with no large scars or defects.

Initially Pud revealed a more likable, human side of himself, but after a few minutes of his excitement, he seemed to shake loose from his out of character mode and reverted to his usual state of cold arrogance.

To avoid having to spend extra time back at the lodge fussing with close fleshing of the hide, I took my time peeling it close to the skin, leaving minimal fleshing to do later. I left the paws and head in the skin and after about thirty minutes of walking with the trophy on my pack board, we were at the lodge. The others were in the living room removing leaves and stems from their berry harvest. They were amazed at what we had collected that fine day. Lars was ready to go immediately for his bear, but I told him that would have to wait at least overnight.

This had been almost too easy, but I cheerfully take 'em as they come.

Not every day will be spectacular. The next few days seemed to drag on. Such is hunting, and such life.

Pat and I were rising about seven or eight each morning, just as light was breaking over that valley located one hundred and fifty-five miles north of the Arctic Circle. Over the decades we had learned that big game animals don't start showing up until around eleven in the morning, but due to time

Three Dutchmen Take Three Big Bears

Pud, pleased with his big grizzly.

manipulations by the government, solar midday arrived at around three o'clock in the afternoon. For solar time one had to set clock time back by three hours.

Lars and Pud wanted to start the day early as they were accustomed to doing in Europe. I explained the difference between clock time and solar, or real time, but they seemed unconvinced. So we accommodated their wishes by starting everything three hours earlier. After enduring several chilly mornings, they told me that leaving the lodge by eleven or so would be fine. They made it sound like it was their idea.

One day as we were about to depart, I went back upstairs and spotted a large grizzly in a berry patch across the river and about a mile downstream from the camp.

Emma announced that she preferred that Lars have a chance to shot before her, so Lars, Pud, and I set off at a brisk walk. The bear was concentrating on slurping up as many of the frost covered berries as it could. We sneaked through the willows on our side of the river until opposite the bear. A gentle breezed drifted down the valley giving us a cross wind approach.

After an hour of slow, careful stalking we were within about one hundred yards of the feeding beast. I placed Lars on a large bump in the tundra and he shot well. The bear immediately charged off to the north, but stopped to bite at its right shoulder. I told Lars to shoot again and be ready to keep shooting, lest the animal gain the thick cover of the next string of willows. The next shot was a miss, which put the bear back in high gear, still headed for the willows a few yards ahead. Lars' third shot rolled the bear and it stayed in place.

We stayed in our position and watched the dark form of the bear for more than ten minutes. Seeing no movement we approached the animal and when close, I moved in front to look at its eyes. The eyes were open, staring off into space. It was dead.

Lars and Pud joined me and we congratulated Lars, then made photographs before I began the skinning. Once again, I took my time so that back at the lodge I would only have to remove the paws and head which usually took me only about one hour.

Two exceptional boars within about a mile of the lodge in a week was remarkably good success. This bear too was well furred with only some small scars around the head. Boars fight a lot, especially in the spring and we usually see large muzzle and facial scars, but not on this one.

That afternoon I was working in the shop on the feet and head when Pat came out to talk to me. She was incensed at the rudeness Lars had displayed in the kitchen - HER kitchen.

I had filleted two salmon and Pat placed them in the oven to bake. When she came back upstairs carrying two buckets of fresh creek water, Lars had removed the fish from the oven and was cutting them into small pieces, planning to prepare them in his preferred way.

Well, I dropped the head and went to the lodge - irate and still in my rain pants which I wore to minimize blood and smell on my britches.

Pud was sipping some of our wine, uninvited, and glared at my interruption, and in such uncivilized attire. I walked right up, too close perhaps, but I was now in my provocative mode, glared into his eyes and told Lars that if he preferred that we prepare fish a different way, or if he wanted to cook the dinner, the proper way to do that is to suggest it, then wait for Pat's approval. No matter what country he was from, his action was rude and unnecessary. But with this pair of overly indulged men, rudeness was routine.

Three Dutchmen Take Three Big Bears

Lars' grizzly was a bit bigger than that of Pud, and squared eight feet three inches.

"Now, would you like to prepare the dinner?" I asked.

Lars seemed like a disciplined kid as he asked if it was okay to cook dinner for all of us.

"You can prepare any meal, but you must make your request and wait for our approval, my friend," I informed him.

"What do you plan to offer with the fish?"

He said aardapel would go nicely, so I got a bag of potatoes for him before I returned to the shop.

Pat thought I should take the two men outside and give them each a whipping. I told her that would be pleasurable for me, but it would not be a good idea. I added that Mr. Lars could bloody well peel or otherwise prepare the potatoes to his liking and that she should remain with me in the shop, with periodic trips back to the lodge to check on what mischief our guests might be making. My sister was boiling mad at these people's behavior, especially in view of how well we treated them, like all our guests, and how well the hunting was going.

We had seven more days to endure the company of these ill-mannered aliens.

Dinner that evening was tasty but the atmosphere was strained. Very little discussion took place and we all retired early.

In the morning Emma emerged first and was smiling. She said she would now like to shoot a great bear, one even bigger than those of the men. I told her that I hoped that would come to be.

The next two days we saw only scattered bands of caribou, most of which were made up of cows with calves.

Lars had begun helping himself to my reading glasses, so on several occasions I would remove them from his face, wipe them off and put them on. When I was finished I put them in places where I thought he would not find them, but he was persistent and did locate them each time. His cheekiness was disgusting, but his companions seemed to not be bothered in the least. These people did not share many cultural values with my sister and me, or anyone else I had ever known.

One morning we saw several small groups of caribou moving down the valley on the far side of the creek. That is the west side and has the most difficult walking of the entire valley. Pud wanted to pursue a caribou, so I sold him a tag and the two of us set off. I carried my meat pack board and rifle, he took his rifle.

As we sat on Two Mile Ridge glassing the valley we noticed five caribou running our way at top speed. Behind the caribou came two large grey wolves in hot pursuit. Pud got very excited and I tried to calm him down. I said we should stay in place and hope for a shot. The frantic caribou passed below us about one hundred fifty yards with the wolves about fifty yards behind. As Pud got ready, resting on a rock, he accidentally discharged his rifle and the wolves turned around and ran the opposite direction. I just smiled at the frustrated, embarrassed Pud. The first wolf was at no trophy fee, so his fumbling just saved me from some extra work. Plus Pud would

Three Dutchmen Take Three Big Bears

Pud with his caribou.

have had to use his caribou tag on the wolf, as he had refused to purchase a thirty dollar wolf tag. That would have necessitated our return to the lodge to purchase another tag before we could go on for a caribou.

We were near Popple Creek and about five miles from the lodge when Pud finally got a chance to shoot a bull caribou. It had a respectable rack - not an outstanding set of antlers - but it was the best we had seen.

The next day more caribou were coming down the west side of the valley and Lars got a chance to shoot at a really magnificent bull at one hundred yards, but he missed - five times.

Neither of the Dutchmen were very talkative that evening, but Emma was effusive in her enthusiasm to take a big grizzly.

With two days left before the Dutch were scheduled to depart, Lars, Pud, Emma, and I walked down to the South Overlook, about three and a half miles from the lodge. Greta stayed with Pat to pick more berries. The day was clear and warmer than any previous day of the booking.

We ate our lunches and as the others took a nap, I saw a lone grizzly across the river browsing near the base of a rocky cliff at the base of the mountain.

As I woke the others up, I saw another large grizzly below the first bear. They were about a mile and a half from us and I suspected we had a sow with a large cub, but the lower bear saw the other and gave chase. When the higher bear became aware of its status as prey, it began climbing as fast as it could up into the rocky cliffs. The top bear would pause to rest when the large one stopped, then the chase resumed as they rapidly gained altitude.

It was time for us to hustle over to see if Emma could get a crack at the larger bear. I kept track of the two critters until the top one went over the skyline into sheep country. The lower bear stopped and rested before it began its descent back toward the valley floor.

We covered the mile or so in record time and were sitting in a patch of willows below the descending grizzly which was taking its time as it continued coming right toward our position.

When the brutish bear was about eighty yards uphill from us and in the clear I told Emma to shoot for the middle of the chest. She fired, her shot was low and to the left of her intended target. She hit the bear in the right front foot. Without pause the beast came right at us. It seemed to have us in sight and was hell-bent to beat us up. Emma fired again, but missed the bear. Pud fired, but his muzzle was close to Lars' head and Lars was rolling on he ground moaning that his ear had been shot out.

A reflexive glance at Lars revealed no blood, so I took aim and hit the bear in the chest, but it kept coming. Then Emma, Pud and Lars all joined me in the shooting. I hit the bear two more times in the chest and some of the other's shots actually connected with the enraged brute. It stopped about twenty yards uphill from our position and was still at last.

This bear was larger than the last two by a noticeable amount. It had been hit nine times. The right foot was broken, two more shots were in the right foreleg, but did not break a bone, my three shots were in the chest, each hind leg took a bullet - one of which shattered the left knee joint and one bullet had creased the rump.

This was a grizzly kill the like of which gives *Ursus horribilis* the reputation for which it is so well known and clearly deserves. To say they can be very hard to kill, is an understatement.

Lars posing with Emma's bear.

I was still using a film camera and the only picture of that giant grizzly that came back from the developer was the one with Lars. And it was no surprise our Dutch guests did not mail me any photographs from their country.

By my reckoning that huge bear had been chasing the other bruin with the intention of either eating it or running it out of the dominant bear's territory. It was hot, tired, and disgusted when the first bullet bit its foot. That was enough to anger, rather than intimidate, the big fellow and he was determined to come down and whoop up on whatever antagonist or victim he could reach.

It's my belief that all predators have a temper, which sets them apart from prey species, and that adrenalin-fueled temper is a key to what makes them so difficult to kill, unless they are completely unaware of the first shot and it is immediately disabling.

We dragged our feet back to the lodge after dark. This time I was tired from packing the bear skin. Lars complained that his ear was still ringing from Pud's careless shot. Put offered that Lars shouldn't have been standing so close. I made no comment at the time, but it is the shooter's responsibility to not deafen the ears or risk hitting another hunter. In Pud's case, he displayed no feeling for anyone but himself, making him a dangerous companion.

The next day was another beautiful one, so as I finished preparing the skin of the last bear, we filled out single day fishing licenses for each of the four and Pat took the Dutch people to the main river and watched as they flailed their lures about for Arctic Char and Greyling. The women and Lars all caught a few fish, but Pud was unsuccessful. He frequently overcast to place his lure in bushes, stumbled in his ire at the equipment which did not do his bidding, etc. However he had success in breaking one of my rods and its reel. It was obvious to me that his nasty temper was the cause of the broken equipment. It was a used rod of course, so I did not present him with a bill. That just wasn't worth the hassle.

Two Florida hunters were due to fly in with the first charter that would take the Dutch to Kotzebue, but I had trophy fees to collect before the guests got to town where they would be less easy to access. Pud offered Dutch guilders in payment. I refused to accept them, pointing out that our signed contract called for payment in cash, in U.S. dollars at the lodge. Pud assured me that any bank would accept guilders. I was growing more than tired with this officious jerk and told him that I didn't know the exchange rate. He said that he knew, but I said I would not accept his word and if the payment was not made in full, I would retain their firearms and luggage until I received full payment and, furthermore, he would have to pay for storage and shipment of any items I felt it necessary to seize.

On the day of departure Pud announced that he would ride with me in the cub, then make the payment before the afternoon charter came in for the rest of the group. I agreed to that.

We went to the local Wells Fargo branch and to my amazement, the teller told me that indeed, they could exchange guilders for dollars and did so. But Pud, using his exchange rate, was more than a couple thousand dollars short. I suggested that he use his credit card to make the payment complete. Pud withdrew enough to cover the amount due, showing his sour demeanor, as usual.

Not wanting to spend any more time with Pud, I dropped him off at the hotel and grabbed a sandwich for myself at the local grocery store before meeting the Florida fellows to take to the charter.

Pat told me that she had enough of rude hunters and wanted to come out on either charter and go back to Kodiak, so I agreed and warned the Floridians that they would have to choke down the swill that I concocted. They were long time friends and just laughed.

So the Dutch spent another night in beautiful Kotzebue and I went to the airport for their departure, only because I had to get Pat to the jet. The wives hugged me, Lars shook my hand, but Pud looked away. Fine!

Three weeks later when I was back in Kodiak I contacted Ludy with the lurid details of the booking and told her that I was sure the "clients" would complain, but she said she had heard nothing. I was surprised once again by this group of misanthropic, rude people.

Clearly each of the six of us, our four guests, my sister, and myself had been shaken and stirred in one form or another on this hunt.

Cabin Protective Measures

Back in 1975 a small female Grizzly tore off a section of plywood siding in its effort to enter our little twelve foot by twelve foot cabin. I shot the invading bear when it was inside the little cabin - the first time I fired at a distance of about eight feet, but my barrel sighting was a tad off, and the bear, though fatally injured, did not drop. That story is detailed in Toklat Comes A'Knocking.

My wife and I were certainly shaken and stirred.

With the recollection of that uniquely stimulating morning arousal as my primary motivation, I added a second course of five-eights inch T-111 plywood to the walls of the little shack. If, in the future, a Grizzly decided to join us inside the cabin, I figured we would have more time to prepare an appropriate welcome.

Over the course of my, by then, less than ten years in rural Alaska, I had seen some terrible results of bears gaining entry to bush cabins and lodges. One common thread I observed was that bears seldom departed by the same route they used to enter - usually they left separate entry and exit holes in the building.

Fortunately most cabin break-ins took place while the structures were unoccupied by their human owners. Extended periods of vacancy are common to bush abodes. Many cabins sit devoid of human occupation for many months, in fact, most such shelters are vacant for most of the year. So I thought long, hard and often about how might one most effectively protect their shelter when no one, except bears, wolves, and wolverines, were around.

One evening an inebriated local told me that he had his revenge on a neighbor he didn't care for, by rubbing bacon grease all over the walls of the neighbor's cabin. Predictably enough, the smells attracted a bear which proceeded to tear it's way into the cabin and destroy everything inside. Then beast busted a ragged hole in another wall to escape. Subsequent to the original bruin visit, other bears, birds and an assortment of other wild critters had enjoyed the diversion of visiting the open shack and using the unfortunate fellow's cabin as an indoor lounge and latrine.

I was interested in the drunk's story and hoped that I would never be considered to be his enemy ... and that he would never know of the whereabouts of my cabin.

It must be mentioned that no food in a form that emits odors should be left in any unoccupied building, however sealed cans and jars are okay, and glass jars are resistant to breakage by bears. If blood, fish slime, or other smelly things are spilled on the floor or counter tops, one should thoroughly scrub away the spillage and rinse the area with a strong chlorine or lysol solution to kill any smells that might attract a bear.

The same holds true for aircraft and other vehicles. I've seen bush planes with the dried blood of game animals clearly visible on the outside. The blood got smeared on the plane as fresh meat was being loaded into the cabin. I've seen the interior floor of aircraft caked with dried blood, which in addition to being a bear attractant is highly corrosive. I've seen about a half dozen bush planes badly damaged by bears, and in one case by village dogs, as they tore into the aircraft in search of the source of the attractive smells.

As a means of preserving their bush accommodations I'd heard of cabin owners hanging plastic containers such as lye or Easy Off oven cleaner on their cabins in expectation of potential animal miscreants biting into the attractants, and upon experiencing the caustic chemicals in their mouths, they would cease in their attempts to vandalize the premises. But the thought of causing such un-necessary pain and suffering to the beasts was objectionable to me, so I never used any such chemicals.

I've seen bush cabins with sharpened nails protruding from boards tacked over windows and doors, but from all the bear hair on the nails, it was plain to me that the bruins enjoyed using the nails as back scratchers, before ripping them off the structure. The nails didn't grow that hair.

Nailing together a pair of boards in an "X", then placing them in strategic places near the cabin with sharp nails sticking skyward may have dissuaded some bears from frequenting some premises, but often the very people who built the simple counter measures stepped on their own devices, especially when visiting the cabin when the bear "traps" were covered by snow or leaf litter. Often such nailed devices were found scattered some distance from the cabin, only to be discovered by an innocent visitor when he was forced to extract the nail from the plantar surface of his foot. So, overall, these devices did not appeal to me as a preferred and effective form of bear insurance for cabins. One should avoid being hoisted on one's own petard.

Moth balls have a repellant effect on most animals, so I tried festooning my cabin with strips of canvass with moth balls taped on both sides. I suspect that may have been effective, but the strips would only last for the first assault by the bears. I needed something that would endure repeated bear attempts and moisture for months.

Bears tend to revisit anything in their territory that is unusual - such as a cabin or even a large rock sitting on a hillside or in flat country. These objects attract the bears' curiosity and commonly show signs of bruins coming by to rub themselves on the outstanding feature. In one valley in northwest Alaska the U.S. Army left a large single axel trailer on a bench overlooking a stream. I was told the trailer was taken in by a tracked machine in winter, then abandoned back in the 1950s. Several times I landed my super cub on the bench and noticed the trailer had grown hair, so on two occasions when bears were playing hard to get, I camped near the trailer and each time the effort produced a trophy grizzly for the hunter who accompanied me. That valley held very little of nutritional value to draw a bear, but the trailer seemed to keep them coming back.

One fall I neglected to secure my wheelbarrow in the building. When I returned the following spring, bears had gnawed the handles and ripped apart the rubber tire. I decided that hanging a tire in the willows near the cabin might be a worthwhile diversion for bears to occupy their curiosity and time, rather than raiding my buildings. The old tire has been chewed and batted around for years, but still hangs by the steel cable. Think of tires suspended by chains in gorilla cages.

Creosote smells awful. I never tasted the stuff, but I've no doubt that it is more disagreeable to the tongue than it is to the nose. I've built all my stuff in the Arctic using a post and beam foundation and I had a five gallon pail of creosote for treating the ground pads upon which I set the posts to keep the building above ground level. I once saw a Grizzly sniff a treated piece of lumber, then shake its head and run away. So I poured an ounce or so of creosote into a plastic syrup bottle and hung it from a wire near the cabin, hoping other bears would react in similar fashion. It was summer time and when I returned a week later, the bottle had been bitten, but nothing else was disturbed. Before my next departure I hung as many "creosote bombs" as I had empty plastic jugs to fill, and hung them on the cabin and from nearby bushes.

Upon my next visit to the home site I immediately checked out my offerings and found that several had been bitten, one had been chewed and the remainder still hung in place. So, anticipating my liberal use of the preservative, I ordered twenty gallons of creosote to be shipped on the next barge from Seattle.

That proved to be a good idea when a few years later, I could not locate any retail source of creosote. The federal government had reportedly deemed creosote to be too dangerous for the general public to access. Well, I was certainly pleased that I had acted as I did, when I did, and avoided the unwarranted, unwanted governmental protection. And, by golly, I've not only survived after avoiding our nannie government's ill-conceived act (for our own good, always, of course), but my life has been so much simpler and better due to my avoidance of Uncle Sam's protection regarding the use of creosote.

All entrance doors on my buildings are hung so they open to the outside. When large bears thrust their considerable bulk at the door, it would be more susceptible to a break-in if it opened inward.

I covered all building corners with angled steel roofing to prevent the easy access for the bears to gnaw or grip with their claws.

All our combustible garbage gets burned in the trash incinerator, while biodegradable garbage is dumped at one location about a half mile from the lodge, and all empty cans are taken to town on a regular basis. We avoid leaving smells that would entice a bear.

We also avoid leaving our unnecessary "foot prints" on the pristine area we use and love.

For the next thirty-nine years - until 2014 - I had no significant bear depredation at our home site, which by 1981 had grown to a two-story

Before and after a bear sampled the kresote jugs.

main lodge, the partially two-story "guide shack" and a third building which houses a shop and sauna. I attribute the lack of bear damage to the fact that I was "bear-thoughtful" when I constructed the buildings and that every year I hung dozens of creosote filled plastic containers on the buildings and from nearby willows, along with other preventive measures. When I returned each of those thirty-nine years after up to ten months of sitting unattended, I found most of the creosote containers destroyed, but nothing more than a few scratch and chew marks on the wooden buildings.

Additionally, all ground level windows are tightly shuttered. If a curious bruin can detect any motion when it claws at a closure, it will be encouraged to keep at it until it opens the inadequately secured place. On the doors of the two smaller buildings I wedge a small piece of a green willow stick between the hinge and the outer section of the hasp which allows no motion when I test it by pulling on the handle. The steel entrance door of the two story main building, with a large dead bolt, is as tight as a refrigerator door when closed and locked.

If one is unwilling to take these precautions, they should be prepared for major damage.

But in 2014 our long history of freedom from bear damage was shattered ... big time.

A Toklat Grizzly Comes A'Knockin'

In my yard in Kotzebue during the winter of 1974 I precut a small twelve foot by twelve foot plywood cabin to fly up to Trail Creek. We'd been using a canvass wall tent with a wood stove upon which we cooked, and we dried our clothes from lines placed above the stove. We also put up a couple of smaller tents for sleeping. We were content with that, but grizzly bear (*Ursus arctos*) encounters were becoming more frequent and the bears seemed to be getting more cheeky and troublesome with each passing year. If a bear decided to really give us a hard time, we'd be much better off in any cabin than the best of tents. The solid walls would give us better protection from the frequent cold and blustery winds as well.

I began to haul some of the materials in with my Cessna 180 for which I had wheel/skis for winter use, then I got access to the local Civil Air Patrol's Beaver on wheel-skis for personal trips. All I had to do was provide the fuel and oil. At twenty-five gallons of eighty octane gas and usually a quart of oil per hour, it was a very economical way to haul the building materials. Using the CAP Beaver was a side benefit for being in the CAP and being a "checked out" Beaver pilot. That was a reasonable perk for being on call and serving on numerous official searches in the region, often using my own aircraft, and always providing my own fuel and oil.

The frozen bog next to the cabin site provided a smooth two thousand feet of landing strip for a ski plane, whereas the main wheel strip I used during the snow free time, was at that time only nine hundred feet long. Both were adequate for a Beaver, but at my experience level, I wanted all the runway I could get, and a single Beaver load allowed me to get the bulk of the plywood and two by four lumber to the bog.

Kotzebue C.A.P Beaver at a remote cabin on a search. PHOTO BY WARREN THOMPSON.

I landed and stacked the building materials onto a high spot in the frozen cranberry bog only a short walk from the cabin site while good snow cover remained in mid April. I lashed the stack of materials together with ropes. I figured it would keep just fine until I could use the wheel plane strip in June or July.

So, two months later - in early July, using my Cessna 180, I got my wife, Mae, daughter Sandy, and sister, Pat, to the home site. I went back to town for one more load of materials and tools. It's about an hour each way from Trail Creek to Kotzebue in a Cessna 180, and by the time I flew the ninety minute return in my Piper Super Cub with some twelve foot lumber tied to the wing struts, the girls had all the materials packed over to the place we had selected to erect the cabin. We were ready to assemble the first wooden shelter in the history of the world on Trail Creek.

Each of the pieces was numbered, making it quick and easy to assemble the little shelter. We four got it nailed together with the roof on in a few hours, and we slept in the brand new cabin that same night.

The following day we put on the rolled tar paper roofing and installed the windows, door, and stove. My right hand was plenty sore from driving

On the main runway, a prime, fat bull for meat in July.

so many nails. I doubted I could fly the airplane without marked discomfort, but a few days would pass before I had to fly.

We were done in time to take advantage of a large group of caribou coming north and Pat shot one velvet antlered bull on the runway for meat.

Only in Alaska, I figured.

We had booked a couple of sheep hunters for mid August. The two of them and I were a bit crowded, but well served by the new cabin. We saw seven grizzlies during the sheep pursuits, so the guests were pleased to be sleeping behind solid walls. It sure beat the tents.

In late August Pat was back in Kodiak teaching school, but I had taken Mae and Sandy up to the new cabin, enjoying its comforts and security in the wild country. A scheduled meeting had necessitated a trip to Kotzebue which I made, and upon my return, I saw Mae and Sandy on the roof of the cabin with a small fire smoking in a ring of stones situated a few feet from the front of the door. I flew a couple of circles around the site and saw them both waving their arms. They seemed to be pretty excited.

I wondered what was up.

After my landing, I taxied the Cessna to its tie downs and was surprised to not see the gals come running down to greet me and help lug the materials to the cabin. So I carried a load of supplies up the trail, along with my ever present rifle, slung on my shoulder. When I got to the cabin, Mae and Sandy were still perched on the roof and they immediately asked if I'd seen the bear.

However, I had not seen any life form, except the two of them, appearing to be doing calisthenics on the roof.

The story was, they were picking blue berries on the nearby hillside when a blond Grizzly appeared and after seeing them, decided to come closer. They beat a hasty retreat across the swamp, followed by the bear. Mae used a 30:30 at the time and always carried it - everywhere she went. She could shoot very accurately, and knew when not to shoot, as well.

When the two got to the cabin, they went right up the ladder with their berry buckets - straight to the roof top they went, pulling the ladder up behind them as well. That was good thinking. The bear was soon in the yard. Their shouts did not affect the Grizzly, other than to draw its resentful stare, but after nosing around, slapping the wood pile, and knocking over some gas cans, the beast went back into the willows, then headed toward the hillside. Mae told Sandy to keep a watch on it as she went down the ladder and built a small fire in preparation for cooking supper.

For no apparent reason the bear lifted its head, sniffed in their direction and came on a run back to the cabin. Mae went right back up the ladder and again pulled it back up on the roof with her. The ladder on the roof insured a safe descent, and re-ascent if necessary, more than prevention of it being used by the bear, though since that time I have seen bears easily climb a ladder as well as use their teeth and claws to climb up the legs of our "A" frame meat rack near the main lodge.

About an hour after their second time of being "roofed" by the more than intrusive bruin, I came in with the plane. The bear was still in the yard, having walked around the cabin several times, clawing at everything, biting at the corners, and glancing up at the noisy humans on the roof. It was oblivious to the curses and shouts from the ladies above.

Mae and Sandy could not understand how I had not seen the bruin. I couldn't figure that one out either.

We were all extra cautious for the duration of that stay at the cabin, but none of us saw that bear again for the remainder of the season.

Our new cabin got a lot of use the following winter while I used it as a base from which to hunt wolves. We spent several short sessions there that summer and of course we based at our new bush shack for guided and personal hunts that fall. After having it less than a year, I was planning to put an addition on it as soon as practical. We needed space inside to accommodate a couple of hunters along with Mae and me.

Rude Awakening

Early one September morning in 1975, between booked hunters, Mae and I were alone and sleeping in the cabin. I suddenly awoke from a nightmare about a bear hitting a punching bag - you know - the little bag that fighters use to coordinate their staccato jabs and punches. I woke up to hear the cabin being pummeled rapidly - it was not a dream! When I raised up to look out the window, the nose of a blonde Grizzly was about a foot from my own.

The sight of me seemed to enrage the bear and it slapped the glass, breaking the window. I leaped out of the bed and grabbed my rifle. The bear had gone to the far corner of the cabin, less than ten feet from the foot of our bed, where it hooked its claws between pieces of plywood siding and was pulling a section of the outside wall off! Wood was cracking and nails were squealing as the panel was wrenched and jerked off the wall studs.

Mae squealed, too.

In seconds that section of wall was gone and the bear was on its way in. This bruin was clearly determined to make mayhem. From about six feet away, I quickly aimed at the invader's chest -barrel sighting - and fired. The bear withdrew. I heard a clatter as the wounded bear ran into a stack of empty five gallon gas cans about twenty feet from the door. With a shell chambered and safety off I was out the door in my undies, looking for a clear shot to dispatch the marauding grizzly. But the thing had disappeared into the dense willows that surrounded the cabin.

Seeing some large splotches of blood on the ground, I went up the ladder and climbed onto the roof.

It seemed to take half of forever, but actually after only a couple of minutes of visually searching I saw the badly wounded grizz struggling as it made its way across the swampy bog. I was on the roof, so I slid down

Mae with the troublesome Toklat.

the ladder and ran to the edge of the bog in time to put another bullet into the bear. The small blonde female Grizzly collapsed at the base of the hill.

It was certainly a stimulating way to begin the day. After going half naked to be sure the bear was dead, I returned to the cabin for coffee and some snacks. After a short time I felt a chill so I put my pants and shirt on before we set up for skinning the bear. It measured a bit less than six feet squared, and was a young female. She had a blonde hide with dark legs and a dark line down the middle of her back - she was a beautiful example of a Toklat grizzly.

Over the years I've had multiple opportunities to see the damage done to the interior of cabins that had been invaded by bears that busted in when the owners were absent. I wanted to avoid such an inconvenient and expensive mess in my own place, so I asked more experienced people, listened to old timers and checked out scuttlebutt in my effort to secure our tiny shelter that sat one hundred and fifty miles north of the Arctic Circle. I wanted to keep our place as pristine a family chapel as possible.

The little sow grizzly made her own door.

Repairing the damage was easy since I had some partial sheets of plywood and other materials stored under our bed. But I'd built the place using three/eights inch low grade plywood, which was all that was available in Kotzebue at the time. So I resolved to bring up enough five/eights inch high grade material to add a full second course to the walls. It was ordered from Seattle for the next season.

That cabin has not been entered by anyone or any animal but us and our guests since 1975, though I leave it unlocked in our absence in case someone needs an emergency shelter.

A Chronicle of the Second Bear Break-In

In 2014 our Dall sheep season had been closed due to a sudden, huge drop in the sheep population throughout the western Brooks Range in my area, Game Management Unit 23. The sheep numbers had dropped in the areas close enough to Kotzebue for winter and spring subsistence hunters riding snow machines to take animals that, without subsistence rules, would not be subjected to hunting pressure after September 20. But the lodge sits one hundred and eighteen miles north of town and that was distant enough to discourage snow machiners from visiting to hunt.

By 2012 the sheep population on Trail Creek had risen to the highest numbers I had seen during my use of the area which began in 1968. I counted more than one hundred Dall sheep one day from the lodge windows and twenty-two were adult rams. Then, during the winter of 2012-2013 a series of unusual climatic events took place that resulted in heavy ice forming over the snow cover, making access to food difficult to impossible for sheep and caribou. Biologists determined that many of both species starved and many more were so emaciated and weakened that they fell easy prey to wolves and bears. So all hunting of sheep was stopped by the Alaska Department of Fish and Game in that part of the state in 2014.

Prior to the season I penciled out the cost of the aircraft annual and expenses to get it to Kotzebue and back. Normally it takes about ten days to get from Kodiak to Kotzebue. I load my pick-up on the ferry in Kodiak then off-load in Homer and make the five hour drive to Anchorage. Some supplies are best purchased from the big stores in Anchorage such as Costco or Sam's Club, so I do some shopping. Then I motor on up to Fairbanks - another seven hour drive.

The Super Cub annual usually takes only a day or two, but every two years I have to take my Biannual Flight Review and check ride with a certified "check pilot", before making the four hundred and forty mile trip to Kotzebue in the cub. That flight takes an average of six and a half hours. Some years, due to smoke from forest fires or adverse weather I have to wait for several days to depart Fairbanks. All time spent away from home is costly.

So, as I was doing the annual on the super cub, after mulling over the poor economics of the year. I decided to complete the annual on the aircraft, hang a FOR SALE sign on it, and fly commercially to Kotzebue, then I'd use an air taxi to charter in and out of the lodge. This would save me thousands of dollars in insurance and fuel, and several days in travel time on both ends of the trip. With a fresh annual, the Cub would be easy to sell and I would end my flying career which began in 1967. I agonized over selling N3421P which I had owned since 1973 and was the best performing aircraft I had ever flown, but it seemed like the time to do so.

I arrived in my old "home town" just before six o'clock on the evening of August 27. Ron, my friend and by then, also a Registered Guide, got in on August 26. Everything in my old sod shack in town was in decent order.

The next day Ron and I set about organizing food and materials to take to Trail Creek. I had one German, Heinrich, booked, who did not speak English, so I had boned up on my Deutsch with my "See It and Say It in German" book.

With no sheep hunts booking hunters had been difficult that year and I had only a grandfather named Dennis and his grandson, Jake, from Colorado and Heinrich scheduled for the first period which ran from August 29 to September 10. So I would have my son, Martin and two grandsons come up to hunt on the plane that took the three guest hunters back to Kotzebue.

The three non-resident hunters arrived on the evening jet of August 28. Heinrich had arranged to use my spare .300 Winchester Magnum rifle, but Dennis had shipped his and Jake's rifles and gear via FedEx, which I had explicitly advised him not to do, as that company's services are not good in rural Alaska. Their stuff had not arrived, though it had been shipped more than two weeks earlier.

Dennis told me that he remembered my admonition to not use FedEx, but the agent in Colorado convinced him that the gear would arrive after

Arctic Rivers Guide Service lodge on Trail Creek -155 miles north of the Arctic Circle. Shop/Sauna on Left, Main lodge at center, Guide Shack on Right.

only three days. Nevertheless, after seventeen days, their packages were still somewhere to the south. Dennis took responsibility for the problem and said he would pay for an extra charter trip to the lodge if that became necessary. The Cessna 206 charter rate was $1,350.

Being able to speak slowly in rudimentary German, I had planned to go to the lodge that evening with Heinrich and my English/German dictionary, while Ron would come up the next day with the Coloradans, who would overnight at LaVonne Hendricks' fine bed and breakfast located down the beach from town.

However the absence of the hunting gear forced a change in the plans. I would stay back to help deal with FedEx and Alaska Airlines in Kotzebue the next day.

So, handing my "See it, say it in German" book to Ron, I told him that he would need to accompany Heinrich, and I expected him to be fluent in that language by morning.

Ron replied, "Gee, thanks a lot, boss!"

If the missing gear arrived the next day, we would be in fine shape.

Dystopia at the Lodge

So Ron and the German departed for the lodge at nine o'clock that evening. About ten-thirty Ron called me on the satellite phone from Trail Creek.

"Jake, a bear got in and completely destroyed the place." Ron reported.

"Which place got hit?" I asked.

"The main lodge, and it's totaled, shall we come back on the charter" Ron asked.

"No, just make-do using the other two buildings. I'll up tomorrow afternoon. What shall I bring?"

"Bring everything," Ron suggested.

Rats! Now I had things to think over, but first I sat down and thought how really insignificant all this was, compared to the wonderful blessings of my family's good health, our children's attendance at the University of Alaska in Fairbanks, and so many things of much greater importance.

Thanking God for our blessings, I knew we would overcome this setback at the lodge. It was just another inconvenient bump in the road of a long life.

When the charter pilot, Eric Sieh, came back he told me the lodge was in the worst shape of any he had ever seen, so I should be mentally prepared.

Well, old Murphy was riding with me again! This, the first season in forty-four years in which I did not have my own aircraft available and we had an extensive rebuild to do which would require extra trips to town for supplies, etc.

The next day we received Jake's rifle and gear, but not Dennis' stuff. Dennis decided to remain in Kotzebue to retrieve his gear, while I went to the lodge with Jake and the rest of our supplies. Dennis, who was primarily concerned that Jake would get a chance to shoot a grizzly, decided to remain

A Chronicle of the Second Bear Break-In

Our welcome mat for slumming in grizzly dystopia.

First floor, main room.

Kitchen area.

Jake's bedroom.

A Chronicle of the Second Bear Break-In

Dining Table.

Living Room.

at the B&B and send a radio message to us when his gear arrived, then get his own separate charter to the lodge. It seemed the best alternative to what we had originally planned.

If the gear did not arrive on Saturday, with Monday being Labor Day, it would likely be at least Tuesday before Dennis could join us.

When young Jake and I arrived at the lodge early that evening, we were appalled at the scene. The litter was literally (pun intended) knee deep in places.

The bear, or bears, left a disgusting mess throughout the lodge and yard.

The main room on the ground floor was littered with flour, cake mixes, bear poop and urine. The stove was knocked over and the bedding was ripped to pieces.

The kitchen cabinets were destroyed and the stove was battered and laying on its side.

Ron had been working for nearly a full day by the time I arrived, but his efforts had been mostly spent on making Heinrich as comfortable as possible and gathering up the spare cooking stove, pots, bedding, etc. Only the cast iron pots and skillets were left undamaged. Anyway, he found things in even worse condition than those that greeted me. The bear had bitten every table and counter top, chewed the window sills, shredded the curtains, ripped out interior panelling, and either bit or pooped on every chair, couch and stool. It was not what anyone expected to see.

To my grateful surprise, the main table was left standing.

In the main room, furniture, and walls were a mess. The big window was hanging by a sliver of one wall stud and the caulking. Much of the paneling and insulation had been torn out.

We were relieved to find that the broadcast radio, was still functional. By some miraculous luck, no windows were broken.

Every cabinet and shelf had been pulled off the walls and all the counter tops had been chewed. The floor was piled with broken containers, flour, cake, and cookie mix and topped off with bear urine and feces. Maps and pictures on the walls were ripped and ruined.

The bear had chewed on the window sills and tore at the wall beneath the main window, in its attempt to make an exit route, but it had failed in that effort. I found two Northern Shrikes and one Robin lying dead in the main room. Apparently the birds had entered through the lower doorway and, finding no open exit on the top floor, they perished from starvation and/or stress.

My bedroom had been taken over by a big bear, and he had not been potty trained. A large fecal deposit adorned my pillow.

Most of the furniture was destroyed, and every piece was gnawed and upended. Most of the cushions had been defecated upon, as well as being chewed up.

In spite of all the piles of bear poop, the place did not smell that bad. Apparently the open door and enough time had elapsed to dissipate the odor of bear feces. Also from the looks of the older piles of poop, this mountain bear had apparently been eating grass and berries, rather than meat, which probably partially explained its offal being less smelly and diarrhetic.

Since before coming to Alaska I have kept a daily log and in 1972 I began keeping a separate log book which always remained at the lodge. That hard bound book had been partially eaten. I noticed some of it in a large bruin fecal evacuation which showed some still legible pages - even after passage through the bear's alimentary canal. So with my bare fingers, I read some of my notes from years past. (I want to assure readers that I did not lick my index finger to turn the pages.)

As I sat down on my bed to read some of the old log entries, I felt a sharp stab in my backside. I carefully reached back to palpate the irritant and found I was impaled by several large porcupine quills.

Ron happened to look in to see me as I studied my old notes. He thought I was depressed as I reviewed the mess, until he noticed the script on the damp and discolored sheets of paper I was deciphering.

"Are you okay, boss?" he wondered aloud.

"Oh, I'm fine, just noting that on this same date in 1978 we had high wind, snow flurries and several hundred caribou on each side of the valley. It's disappointing to lose the log entries of the past forty years, but I always made duplicate entires in my annual logs, so all is not lost," I responded.

Nodding to Ron, I motioned to my derriere and said that I needed his assistance and suggested he glance at my backside. He reluctantly bent over to observe the quills. I told him that I would appreciate him yanking them out.

My friend resolved to do his duty, trying to not show his distaste for the unusual chore.

"Grab hold with a pair of pliers, one at a time, and jerk them out, but cut the ends off first, as they are hollow."

De-quilling porcupine-adorned dogs taught me that little trick back on the ranch in Montana. Those three of the critter's hypodermic contributions to my nether region were not lodged too deep into my stern anatomy, but I was somewhat lamed up for a couple of days, reminiscent of having a penicillin injection in the rump. I mentioned that it's a good thing the quills weren't loaded with a filovirus ... like one of the five flavors of Ebola! Yep, it could be worse.

Apparently one or more porcupines (*Erethizon dorsatum*) had entered the lodge after the bear opened it up and had made it "home" for a spell. After being impaled, I noticed quills all over, even small ones, which indicated the critter was running out of dermal darts. It must have enjoyed the comforts of the lodge for an extended stay. Either porcupines are too dim witted to fear bears, or they just don't worry about them. The lodge is well north of the tree line, but we see single quill-pigs nearly every season at Trail Creek. When I had a dog in camp, I used to kill the pestiferous rodents, as dogs seem to be unable to resist fooling with a slow moving porky and the consequences are painful - sometimes even fatal for dogs. But now, with no dog sharing the time with us, we continue to let the porcupines go their own way. From my personal experiences I want to assure readers that porcupines can be a pain in the butt.

An especially obnoxious oder seemed to emanate from Ron's room which doubles as a pantry. After enduring the special stench for several days he began a thorough search which revealed an accumulation of porcupine poop underneath his bed. It was different in appearance from bear scat and far more repulsive in smell. It seemed the critter had established his latrine spot and used it faithfully. I had never whiffed that distinctive flavor of feces before.

That bloody bear would pay dearly for its transgressions, I promised myself and my companions. And I knew that having discovered such a fascinating and tasty bounty, the house breaker would return.

Just how those shed quills were positioned to penetrate my rump when I sat down continues to torture me, but we were to be entertained with plenty more pressing imponderable issues before we finished restoring the lodge to full function.

A Chronicle of the Second Bear Break-In

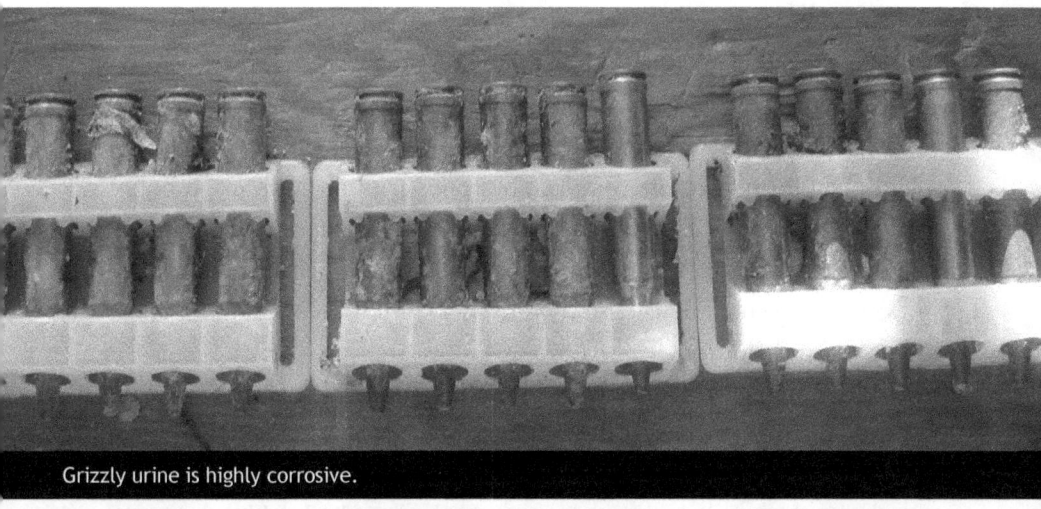

Grizzly urine is highly corrosive.

The stair carpet was beyond restoration or use.

When I arrived I wondered where all the junk had come from. It seemed impossible that so much litter could have been created from what we'd left in the lodge ... but then, I have a hard time throwing anything away, as anyone who knows me is aware. Book and magazine pages in original form are quite compact, but once crumpled, bitten through and, in some cases, making the voyage through the stomach, then the intestines of a grizzly bear, those pages make up into a much larger volume. The same thing could be said for the stuffing of pillows, couch upholstery, rugs, towels and clothes.

Every single cartridge I'd left the fall before -.22, shotgun shells, 30/30, and .300 win mag - was scattered on the floor and horribly corroded. I've seen less arthritic-looking corrosion on brass accidentally left uncleaned after soaking in salt water. Apparently the bear had deliberately urinated on every batch of ammunition it found. Over the next two weeks, usually just before bed time, I spent hours with a brass brush and steel wool cleaning them up so they would chamber. Some rounds had been bitten and bent, so they were not recoverable. I was thinking it was too bad the critter hadn't put a canine on a primer and self destructed.

We began the clean up using snow shovels to rid the building on the clutter on the floor, but we carefully inspected the debris as ammunition was scattered throughout. We planned to burn most of the junk soon after it was collected, before the wind could scatter it. We wanted no live ammunition in the burn pile.

Every aluminum pot and utensil had been bitten and rendered unusable by the bear.

The main carpet in the living room was fouled with bear excrement, but after two rounds of hand shampooing, it was in acceptable condition. The carpeting on the stairs was destroyed beyond restoration, as were the bedroom rugs. The chewed rugs brought to mind a politician's anguished tantrum after loosing an election - maybe like those reported of Hilary Clinton on Nov. 8, 2016.

After more than thirty-four years of nothing but a few chew marks on the corners, a bloody bruin had invaded the lodge and lived there for some time - weeks, I reckon - if poop deposits account for time in service. The *Ursus* beast swallowed every plastic grocery bag and deposited their twisted

A Chronicle of the Second Bear Break-In

remains outside, but dozens of plops were left inside - and my bed had been a favorite depository.

Several dozen poops with twisted plastic bags littered the outdoor surroundings and some of the bags seemed to be tied in knots, but I did not take time to determine if they were square knots, marriage knots, or whatever. I'm sure some of the plastic laced poops will become part of the landscape, remaining in place for years, as we did not have time to organize a search party to completely rid the area of the offal piles outside the lodge. After more than two years I'm still discovering surprise piles.

The cabin bear had left his large front paw print on one of the doors. A combination of coco, cake mix and bear urine served in place of the black ink normally used for fingerprints. It took a huge bear to have a paw that large.

Before I arrived with Jake, Ron had used our tent camping gear and Coleman stove to cook and get by with for himself and Heinrich, and that would have to serve until we could get the cooking stove working.

We got our guests fed, then sighted in their rifles. Once the rifles proved true, we went back into clearing the mess and restoring the various functions of the lodge. Ron and I kept working until well after midnight on Friday.

The downstairs guest bedrooms had received the least damage, so we put them back in decent order for our guests to use. I secured the outside door with rope attached to a bell to alert us if a bear attempted to join us, which I expected at any moment.

As always the outhouse frames had been torn apart, so I re-assembled one, then placed it over a freshly dug hole. I cautioned everyone to carry their rifle with them at all times, even when going outside for a stand-up job, i.e. to pee. This bear had taken possession of the lodge and he would be coming back as surely as a bear returns to a kill site, and it was apt to be aggressive toward us, the intruders, that the bear would view as attempting to take over its newly claimed prize.

A light skiff of snow dusted the area when we arrived and conditions remained overcast with intermittent snow squalls for the next several days.

Saturday dawned with visibility reduced to less than a mile in snow and fog. Conditions remained the same throughout the day.

After a light breakfast I was removing the ruined linoleum and adhesive from the kitchen floor when Ron noticed a bear moving through the berry patches on the foothills east of the lodge. We paused to watch the animal as it fed closer to the lodge. After a few minutes the beast seemed to become interested in the buildings and cautiously approached. This bear did not appear to be as large as the paw print indicated the marauder to be, so as it gingerly stepped around the guide cabin I fired a shot at a rock a couple of feet in front of the bear. The noise and rock shrapnel sent the bear tearing through the willows and away from the cabin. By its behavior and size I was convinced that this was not the perpetrator of our misery. This was a medium sized, sub-dominant bear that probably recognized the smell of the cabin bear. And, it was still one day before bear season opened for non-residents.

We got a lot done that day, but time was passing much too quickly considering all the work we had before us. We paused to eat a meal of deer burger and noodles, along with some store-bought pecan pie, before going back to the cleaning chores.

Well after dark on the night of August 30 wolves howled from close quarters, east and west of the cabins, they left clear tracks in the snow a few feet from the guide shack, but due to the overcast and darkness, we did not see a wolf. The lobos carried on for more than twenty minutes. It was an interesting canine dialog, but we can only guess at the content. No doubt they were familiar with the premises and knew we uninvited spoilers were present. It would have been satisfying to have had an opportunity to shoot some or all of them.

Saturday, August 31 began with the outside temperature at thirty degrees. Inside the lodge it was a more comfortable fifty degrees. The visibility had improved to three miles and the overcast was at 3500 feet.

All of our stored canned goods had been ripped open and consumed. The glass containers were not broken. The ruptured cans and other materials filled four cardboard apple boxes which I got ready to eventually take to the Kotzebue dump.

With the propane cooking stove back in order, we enjoyed baked salmon, potatoes and a salad for dinner. Heinrich informed me that he did not eat fish of any kind, so I opened a can of ham for him. I always ask guests to inform us of allergies or strong food presences, but there was that language barrier issue with Heinrich.

Ron burning some of the combustable garbage.

How our small library and other paper products could have been transformed into such a volume of trash was amazing. The interior of the lodge reminded me of photographs of buildings made shortly after a military shelling, a bombing, or maybe the act of a terrorist.

Monday, the first of September arrived with the outside temperature at plus thirty-two degrees amidst mixed rain and snow with a light and variable wind. Visibility was three to five miles. Snowy, foggy squalls drifted in periodically to envelope our surroundings, only to move on up the valley and temporarily clear the air.

As our guests were not keen on leaving the building in the conditions at hand, after a coffee and oatmeal we went back to the house work. Ron was outside burning another massive pile of garbage as I was scraping tile adhesive and other mess from the floor. Jake and Heinrich were gazing out the windows when a large Grizzly appeared on the eastern foothills. It stood up briefly, then came rapidly toward the buildings. It was oblivious to the garbage smoke that lazily drifted its way.

This bear was on a mission and I was reminded of an irate landlord coming to confront delinquent renters.

I told Jake this bear was about as large an inland Grizzly as he would ever see, so he said he would like to shoot it and asked what we should do.

I told Jake that he should hurry to get his rifle from his bedroom downstairs as I opened the east window of the living room. The bear was coming home and we needed to prepare an appropriate welcome. I waved to Ron to join us inside.

In far less time than I anticipated, the big grizzly walked boldly past the guide shack and was coming directly to the still un-repaired door to the main lodge. I had the clear impression that the bear knew someone or some thing had trespassed on his recently acquired abode and it was going to set them straight, regarding who was in charge. The great best came boldly on, with the deliberate stride of a neighborhood bully, bent on mayhem.

If Ron had remained at the garbage burn he would have been confronted by the disgruntled Grizzly.

I told Jake to hold until I signaled to shoot. When the bear was about four feet from the door, I nudged him and whispered "now". Jake fired his 300 Winchester Magnum. The Griz dropped to the ground.

I told young Jake to put another round into the bear, aiming for the neck just behind the head. The beast absorbed the second shot without a perceptible twitch.

We cut Jake's bear tag, made some photographs, rolled the bear away from the main building and Ron set at skinning the warm carcass as the snow flurries continued. We hung all four quarters on the meat pole. The bear was an old boar, a bit less robust than most for that time of year, but it was not in bad shape.

I was as confident as anyone could be that we had dispatched the marauding bear, but I cautioned everyone to keep carrying their rifle for even the most brief of their outside activities. The population of Grizzlies is high around the lodge and those we eliminate are soon replaced.

Young Jake and the cabin grizzly.

After a light lunch, Ron took young Jake up the creek while I took Heinrich to the eastern foothills to glass for caribou or wolves. Heinrich was only interested in taking a caribou. After a couple hours of sitting in the snow and rain squalls while seeing no movement of big game, we all returned to the lodge. Even a half destroyed shelter is better than none at all.

Bear stew and baked salmon made a nice dinner for all, after which I spent thirty minutes filling out the paperwork for the bear.

Canned whole kernel corn has always been a favorite of mine. This bear had consumed two, twelve-can, cases of corn well before we arrived, so that made him the first and best corn fed grizzly bear that I had ever tasted. And it was good.

Ron and I had the place working well enough and the weather had improved sufficiently for us to start spending some serious time looking for caribou.

On September 2 we awoke to a bit over two inches of new snow on the ground, with steady snow limiting visibility to less than a mile. The temperature stood at twenty-eight degrees and the squirrelly wind was switching from the south to the east at about fifteen, gusting to thirty miles per hour. Those were miserable conditions for bush flying.

Dennis had scheduled a charter trip to the lodge as soon as his gear arrived, but with the Labor Day weekend and all, his stuff had not yet arrived.

I called Eric at Back Country Outfitters and gave him a weather report in case he had other trips to make up our way and asked him to give Dennis some good news - that his grandson had taken a large bear.

Repairing, re-assembling, and hooking up the oil stove downstairs took most of the afternoon, but it functioned as it should and the supplemental heat was wonderful. I had just enough spare stove pipe to replace that destroyed by the grizzly.

So after a hearty meal of baked chicken, corn, green beans and freshly baked brownies we were tired and everyone went to bed shortly after ten o'clock.

Wednesday began with a solid overcast and light snow, which by then was a bit over three inches deep on the runway. We had five miles visibility so Visual Flight Rules (VFR) were in effect. A wind of about fifteen miles per hour was coming right up the runway from the south. The wind and weather conditions were good for a charter trip. I called Eric to report conditions and he confirmed that Dennis had received his gear on the last plane of the previous day.

Around noon the charter arrived with Dennis. His decision to use FedEx had cost him six days of delay and kept him from witnessing his grandson shooting the bear, but he was cheerful about everything.

Suffice it to say, the next several days were frustrating with adverse weather, a paucity of big game and the ongoing demands of restoring the lodge. We saw caribou and more bears, but no more big game was taken.

On September 10, Dennis and Jake departed with the hide and skull of Jake's bear on the charter that brought my son and grandson to the lodge.

The next day Martin spotted eight large bull caribou coming from the south, before they headed into West Bowl. He and Stuart went after them, but were not able to get within range for a shot.

A hot sauna/bath allowed Ron and me to loosen up tense muscles and scrape off a week-old layer of our natural "protective crust". That closed the day for us on a good note.

At breakfast the next morning we heard, then sighted a Northern Three-Toed Arctic Woodpecker. This was the third, the best, and the most prolonged observation of any woodpecker I had experienced in my forty-seven years in the Arctic. The bird was bold and remained an enjoyable distraction to us throughout the day. I had been patching pecker holes in the buildings for the past ten years. I assumed the damage had been done during the winter. This lone bird was persistent and seemed to prefer the kiln-dried T-111 siding to wild wood. I painted some creosote on the top story siding, but that did not seem to bother the "pecker wood". The intrusive, but interesting woodpecker was bent on teasing us the entire day.

My left knee and Stuart's ankle were bothering, but the aches and pains were quickly forgotten when Ron spotted a big bear up north near the mouth of Sea Gull Creek. He and Stuart set off for the bruin. Ron had been helping me at Trail Creek since 2005, but had not taken a grizzly for himself. With no guest hunters in camp to take a grizzly, this was a perfect opportunity for Ron to collect a bear.

When they got to the foraging bear, the best approach was from below as the bear slowly moved around eating berries on a side hill. A second, slightly smaller bear approached from above the feeding animal. The second bear appeared to be stalking the other, but when it was detected, the larger one gave chase and ran the newcomer out of sight, then went back to slurping up berries.

Ron and Stuart ascended a small knoll directly below the bear and waited, but the berry picker spotted the men and came running toward them. It's likely the bear wanted to run the humans away from its garden spot. I assume it figured them to be more, and smaller, bears.

At about sixty yards Ron fired and the bear dropped to the ground, but it still had some control of its motion, as it tumbled toward the pair of hunters, still focused on them, the intruders. At about fifteen yards Ron fed it another 180 grain guided lead missle. The bear bunched up and was still.

Ron showing his "Weatherby Award" from his rifle recoil.

Ron told me that Stuart looked shocked and his complexion was noticeably ashen. This was Stuart's first experience with shooting a bear of any species.

This was a large sow bear with primarily blonde pelage that showed spots of bluish and gray hair. It was a very plush, beautiful hide. The head was blocky, more like that of a boar than a sow. As it was coming down the hill its behavior gave the impression that it was an aggressive male. The well formed, but dry nipples indicated it had cubs sometime in the past, but had not been nursing for years. This was another example of a cranky old sow acting like a dominant boar. I've known some women like that.

The rush of events coupled with the steep uphill angle of his second shot resulted in Ron's receiving a crescent shaped cut over his right eye from the back end of his rifle scope. Bear hunting can be a bloody business.

They started skinning at seven o'clock and were back to the lodge around midnight, and well after dark. In addition to the hide with feet and skull attached, they toted back the hind quarters. This was another "sweet" Grizzly,

A Chronicle of the Second Bear Break-In

The kitchen was looking pretty good by close-up time.

having fed mostly on grass and berries. It's meat would be good. With two people sharing the load, that chore is not too heavy on ether one, although the distance was around five and a half miles.

On Sunday, September 21, the charter came in just after ten o'clock, loaded up Stuart, Martin, Ron's bear skin and meat and most of the other gear to take to town. It was a rush, as is usual that time of year. About one thirty another Cessna 206 came in for Ron, Spencer who had joined us four days earlier, and me. We were in Kotzebue by three o'clock that afternoon.

So ended the slowest hunting season I had seen at Trail Creek in forty-seven years. We took two dandy Grizzlies, saw a total of about twenty Caribou, a few dozen Dall sheep, one Muskox, three wolves, and a few ptarmigan, but we had pretty well restored the badly damaged lodge.

One of the local Transporters after hearing of our lack of caribou remarked to me that he had dropped seventy-eight hunters out and they reported one hundred percent on caribou.

I congratulated the fellow heartily.

But then, laughing as he slapped me on the back, he added that his one hundred percent meant that none of his drop-out hunters had taken a single caribou.

2000, Greg Fischer's Mauling

The Deer Hunts

I met Greg Fischer while on a swap hunt in Wyoming in 1997. My buddy, Tom Dooley was along. As had been the case with almost every other swap hunt I tried, it turned out to be disappointing. The photos the fellow sent to me were of mountain mule deer at high elevations - really big, impressive mulies. It's always best to assume nothing and check everything, but I naively presumed that those bucks were taken in "his area" and that we would be hunting there, too. I later learned that the photos I had been provided were of deer that the "guide" had personally taken and they were harvested hundreds of miles away, in an entirely different habitat from the area we would hunt.

We wound up going to Gillette, out in the prairies. While that is very interesting country, with an abundance of mule deer and antelope, - and salamanders - the deer were not of super trophy quality, to say the least. Driving from the airport to our "hunting camp" which turned out to be a motel - the "guide" told my partner and I that he figured there was no place in Campbell County that he couldn't get to within fifty yards of - in his pickup truck. Then he demonstrated his spotting scope "tripod" which clamped to his rolled down truck window. Just then I realized that I should have spent more time checking this guy out.

Oh, well, we were there and would try to make the best of what came our way from then on.

The best thing about the trip was meeting Greg Fischer, who, upon hearing that a couple of Alaskan guides were coming, had volunteered to help with the hunt. Greg was a serious and competent hunter and a very enjoyable companion. He had operated his own guide outfit in Western Wyoming for over twenty years.

Greg took this buck after the others filled their tags.

First Octopus for the Wyoming guide, Greg on Left.

Our original swap had been for Tom and I to each take a mule deer and the Wyoming fellow was to take two Sitka Blacktail deer. We were so favorably impressed with Greg, that we offered to take him on the Sitka Blacktail deer hunt at no fee, as well.

Greg came to Kodiak for his Sitka deer hunt and brought a pair of paying guests with him, - a very thoughtful thing to do. His performance on the boat and in the field was exemplary. Every evening he sat with halibut pole in hand, fishing while we were at anchor. When I arose to start coffee and breakfast, each morning, Greg was already at the rail, fishing. His efforts paid off, too, as he landed a halibut of about forty pounds and a big octopus, both new species to him and both were cooked up to their usual delicious standards.

Halibut were available, too.

Greg helped the other fellows secure some really dandy trophies, including one that placed number two in the 1997 statewide "Big three" competition, before he shot one for himself. Then, the next season, he returned with another revenue guest and we enjoyed his company once again.

The Arctic Hunts

In the year 2000, or Y2K, I had bunk space available at the lodge during the prime booking period which ran from late August to mid-September and told Greg he was welcome to join us as a non-revenue guest. He offered a swap for elk and a mountain mule deer, but I told him that we should take advantage of this opportunity and worry about me hunting with him whenever it might happen to come together for us both.

He was able to fit the time in with his booking schedule and then found a paying guest, Don, to bring with him. Greg was one good man!

The season began and continued with warm, wet weather. It rained part or all of nearly every day. The creeks and rivers were running high. We'd seen plenty of bears, wolves and dall sheep near the lodge, but caribou - those always unpredictable beasts - were less abundant than usual. The level of wolf activity - plenty of tracks and poop - indicated that caribou were likely around, or on their way.

One rainy day, Greg and his buddy, Don, found a place to ford the overflowing Trail Creek just down from the runway and they got an opportunity to shoot at a large black wolf right there, but the wolf was not hit. The two men continued on down the valley, traversing some of the most boggy, brushy areas in the drainage. About five miles down they sighted a long string of caribou traveling south on the far side of Popple Creek. For a number of reasons they did not shoot one, but noticed that more gangs of caribou were coming out of the mountains in that area, so they resolved to return the next day.

That evening we had a birthday cake for Greg, who turned fifty-five that day. Don was 65 and close to his birthday, so my sister, Pat, made a pair of cakes. I emphasized to them that evening that they needed to stick close together, especially in heavy brush, as our grizzlies normally run away from humans, but some are rank by nature. However, I knew of no instance in which two or more people were ever successfully attacked by a bear. The day had been especially physically tiring for us all, with no one shooting anything. We all turned in early.

The next morning, Greg and Don headed to Popple Creek, crossing at the only fordable place, just down stream from the runway.

Dick, from Honolulu, and I went to the East Moguls to do some serious glassing. Pat stayed at the lodge with Jason, who had pulled a groin muscle the day before. The other hunter, Jason's buddy Lon, remained at the lodge as well.

As Greg and Don topped out on Two Mile Ridge (named for it's distance from the lodge), I could see long strings of caribou walking south on both sides of Popple Creek, which was three miles further from the ridge. That looked good. Greg and Don saw them too, and were spurred on by the prospect of taking a good bull.

Overcast still plagued us, but the conditions were drying up and I dozed off for a short nap.

Sometime after lunch a Grizzly appeared on the alluvial fan opposite the lodge. Soon thereafter, Dick and I observed Pat, Jason and Lon headed that way, crossing Trail Creek the same place that Greg used. We saw the trio stalk within a hundred and fifty yards of the grazing Grizzly, then saw it jump and run uphill. Seconds later the sound of the shot reached us, followed by another report from a rifle.

I've known Jason since he was two years old. His Dad, Bruce, first hunted with me in 1978. Jason, like his Dad, is a very good shot. I wondered if continually being soaked by the rain had warped his wooden stock. Later, we test fired it and that seemed to be the cause of his misses, as it was way off center.

About two o'clock we followed Greg and Don with our binoculars as they entered a riparian area midway to Popple Creek. Shortly after they entered the lower end, a sow Grizzly came busting out of the brush uphill from them, followed by a single cub. The two bears were running hard and turned up into sheep country. As they progressed higher, sheep began appearing ahead of the bears. It brought to mind popcorn exploding from a pan. I'd never before seen bears acting more spooked, or sheep reacting to bears as they did that afternoon.

After another half hour of careful searching for game with my binoculars in my face, I turned to glass down the creek and saw one human figure coming back toward the lodge. The man was hustling. I told Dick that I had a very morbid feeling. I feared that Don had suffered a heart attack and Greg was coming for help.

I slipped into my hip boots and told Dick to meet me at the lodge, I was going to meet Greg at the creek, which by then, had risen to river size.

My fastest continual pace was fifty steps, followed by fifty strides at a trot and I was at the river before the other guy got there. I was shocked to see that it was Don, not Greg!

Don hollered to me, "Greg got hit by a bear and it's real bad. I think he's going into shock!"

I told Don who was worn out, to join me at the lodge as soon as he could and I ran to get supplies. I was going over in my mind where Greg must be lying, as I had last seen the two enter a large willow patch just short of Popple Creek.

The Rescue

At the lodge, I left my jacket, putting on a long sleeved coat liner. I knew that exertion would soon have me too warm and sweaty, setting me up for a serious chill, and I was not going to stop until Greg was back at the lodge. Also a heavy hunting jacket would be an impediment to the haste and exertion demanded by the situation.

Gathering up some spare rounds for my .44 pistol, I thrust them into my pocket and stuffed a small pack with candy bars, a bottle for water, some aspirin/codeine, a length of light rope, some duct tape, a five foot by seven foot blue tarp, two flashlights with extra batteries, and my small handax - a Normark Skinning Ax. As I went down the stairs, I noticed a plastic Stanley mitre box mounted on a piece of 1X4, about four feet long. Not really knowing why, I grabbed that, too.

I scribbled out a note for Pat to come as soon as possible with two thermos bottles of warm soup and all the candy, etc. that she figured the group would need. All should bring a flashlight with extra batteries and a water canteen, while minimizing other superfluous stuff, and follow Don's lead to join me.

But only one person should carry a rifle with a full magazine, and nothing in the chamber. I didn't want a bunch of nervous people with rifles stumbling around in the dark.

As I went out the door, Don and Dick arrived in the yard and I told them to wait for Pat and the other two men, as we would need all the help we could get. Greg weighed about 220 pounds. He was very fit, but now very crippled, and it was going to be a long, tough chore getting him back to the lodge.

Don told me that Greg had shot at the bear twice and thought he hit it both times. Dick and I had not heard any shooting, except for the two shots Jason made.

I ran the 400 yards to the river crossing, then resolved to pace myself to avoid a total, early burnout. I was really high on adrenaline, extremely worried about Greg and completely focused on what was at hand.

Once across the river, I began to run fifty paces, then walk fifty steps, closing the distance between me and my injured friend as fast as I could.

Unable to follow the stream due to it's high water, on my hands and knees, I clawed my way up the first big cut bank and high stepped through the tussocks, stumbling occasionally. It was a relief, and allowed me to speed up when I got out of the soggy marsh and onto solid rock and ground as I climbed Two Mile Ridge. Once on top I paused to carefully look over the area ahead, hoping that I would be able to see Greg - maybe a handkerchief tied on a high bush to mark his location - anything - but I saw no sign, so I struck off at a trot.

More boggy tussocks, some up to waist high, slowed me down as I wove my way through the swampy muskeg, made all the worse by countless new rivulets and springs coming off the side hill.

The East side of the valley is dry and well laced with caribou trails making passage relatively fast and easy, but this, the West side, is a nightmare! Between the swampy bogs, dwarf birch was up to shoulder high and miserable to get through. After about an hour and a quarter of difficult, labored travel I was in the area that I believed Greg must be lying. I hollered, then listened, but heard nothing. I fired my pistol three times, then listened. Still nothing. I began to feel really upset, then counseled myself to calm down and stay focused, as my actions would play a huge part in Greg's survival and hopefully, his recovery with both legs functional.

I'd been saying short prayers since I first heard the bad news from Don and now the supplications were coming to mind and voice after shorter intervals.

"Dear Lord, maintain life for my friend Greg and give us both the skill and strength to do whatever he needs to survive and return to his active, healthy life. Father God, I pray that you grant me the right reactions and lead me to the right decisions. And, please, Lord, lead me to Greg soon."

As per Don's brief description, I was searching the lower end of the lines of willows that came off the western slopes of the mountain, but I went to the end of the brush and still had not located Greg. There was only open tundra between me and Popple Creek, so Greg had to be more to the north, back in the direction from which I had come.

Saying another prayer, I moved further uphill. I was about fifty yards into the tangle of willows, alder and dwarf birch, when after firing another volley of three shots, I heard a low moan. I yelled for Greg and heard another muffled moan.

Greg had dragged himself about forty yards into the brush, afraid that the bear would return to find him in the more open area, and he figured he might hear the bear coming through the denser vegetation, but soon thereafter, he had lost consciousness.

Then I was at his side. He looked up at me and said, "I'm bad tore to pieces, just shoot me, Jake, or give me the pistol."

I tried to act light and unattached as I replied, "What are you talking about, man? I've seen guys really torn up, you're gonna be fine, no big deal, buddy, just help me help you." I was appalled at his condition and appearance, but could not let him see my true feelings. I felt nausea when I saw his grossly rearranged lower leg. I had to fight the urge to vomit, but I was successful in that.

His left leg was bent and twisted at a very abnormal angle from just above the ankle. I knew both the tibia and fibula were badly broken and displaced. From behind, I gripped him under his arms, and pulled him to a sitting position, but his pain was excruciating. I made him eat a candy bar and then had him swallow two aspirin/codeine pills and drink the pint of water, then I went for more water, telling him he had to force candy and water to keep his blood sugar up and avoid shock.

Greg told me that he sure didn't feel like eating anything, but I told he had to do it and even more important, he had swallow plenty of water, too.

I handed him a short piece of green willow to bite on and told him I had to straighten his leg - and it was going to hurt, but we had to do it to stabilized the leg to get him back to the lodge and on to the hospital.

What blood was visible, was all clotted and considering the dirty conditions for the trip back, I figured it best to leave his hip boots on and clean up the injury later, at the lodge. I handed Greg a piece of willow to bite on.

I positioned myself at his heels and slowly pulled his leg straight, then put the mitre box at the break of his leg and, after trimming some of the

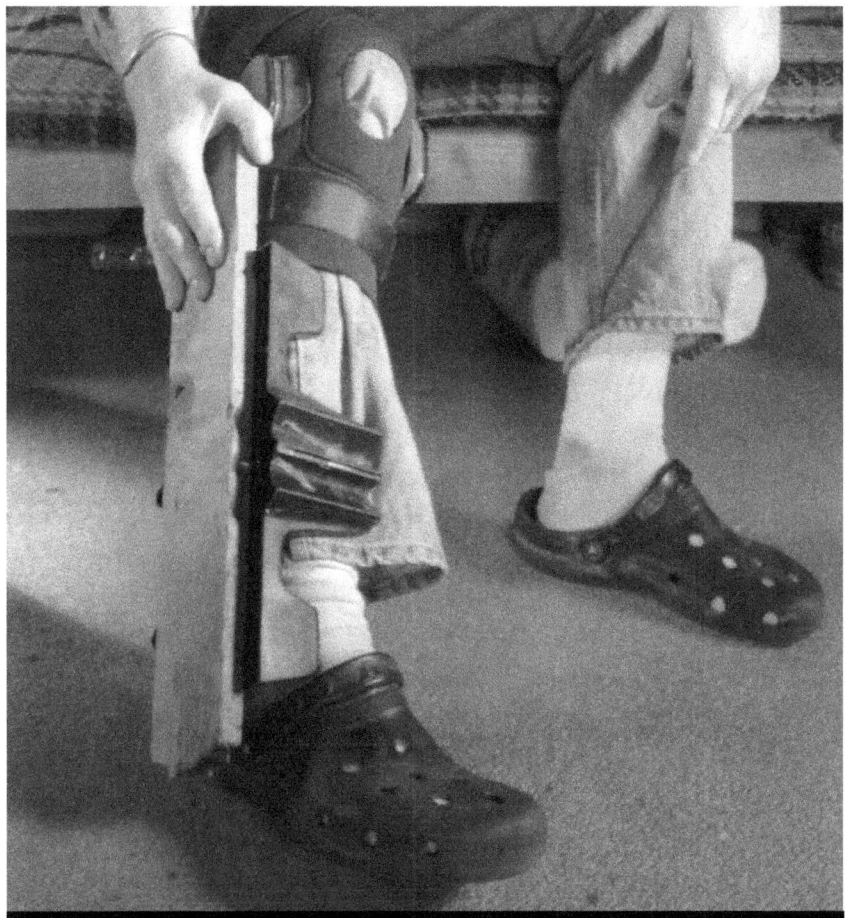

The Stanley mitre box splint as I used it on Greg Fischer.

length from the heel end of the 1X4, I taped the "splint" in place. Greg bit the willow clear through, his head quivering at high frequency, shaking at the intense pain, but he did not make a sound.

It was then that I noticed a large tear and blood on the pant leg of his left thigh.

Later, Greg told me that he had been in a hurry to get to the caribou. Don had lagged too far behind and when Greg looked back, he saw Don step into a clearing just as a big Grizzly stood up, about ten yards uphill from Don, who had not seen the bear.

"DON - BEAR" hollered Greg.

The bruin dropped to all fours and came straight downhill at Greg. The bear was crashing through brush most of the way, but when he got a clear chance, Greg shot and was sure he hit it, maybe striking it a little high as the bear was coming from up the steep hill. But it kept coming and the second shot was point blank into the chest. The Grizzly hit him so hard, Greg did not remember what took place after that.

Don said that he saw the whole thing from less than one hundred yards away and when the bear hit Greg, his rifle flew up fifteen feet into the air and the bear was on him. Grabbing Greg's leg, the bear gave it's head a quick shake, fracturing both the tibia and the fibula, then the beast bit Greg in the thigh, creating a hamburger sized flap.

I've seen bears, wolves and dogs grab an opponent or prey that way. They clamp down on a lower leg, then shake their head which breaks the bones and leaves the other animal severely disabled.

Afraid of hitting Greg, Don aimed his rifle over the bear's back and fired two times before the bear ran off downhill.

The attack had taken mere seconds.

Don was shocked at what he saw. Greg told him to locate his rifle, bring it to him and go for help.

This was about two-thirty in the afternoon. I first saw Don a bit after four-thirty and I departed the lodge shortly before five-thirty to find Greg. I seemed unable to move fast enough. I got to Greg just before seven that evening.

With Greg splinted and the analgesic beginning to kick in, though woefully inadequate for the situation, I loaded him on my back and began to struggle back toward the lodge, but the terrane was rough and wet. His injured foot kept snagging on brush or tussocks, causing exquisite pain. I had only moved him about two hundred yards when Pat, Dick, Don, Jason and Lon hailed us. It was music to my ears.

I cut some willows for a travois and asked Lon to cut some more for walking sticks for each person, as the going was rough and with the solid overcast, darkness was soon going to be complete. I cautioned Lon to be very careful, as the little ax was sharp. Later he mentioned that he was glad I'd told him, as he'd never before seen such a sharp ax.

2000, Greg Fischer's Mauling

We didn't need any more injuries.

Rigging the tarp between the long willows, we began to drag Greg toward home. Willows are very tough, but they're too springy for use as a travois and we soon just wrapped the tarp around an eight foot pole on the top end, had Greg lay down on the tarp and with me and one other man on the front pole, we dragged him through the muck, water and low brush.

In the big tussock areas, I got under one arm and one of the others got the other side and we "hopped" Greg through the miserable stuff. Greg was in terrible pain, his left foot snagging with nearly every step. He kept a willow stick in his mouth to bite, partially muting the pain.

The double aspirin/codeine helped, but he should have had fifteen milligrams of morphine initially and probably another hit or two before we reached the lodge, but I had no morphine. Each time his broken leg got bumped, which was with nearly every move, pain racked his entire being.

During my time in the service which followed a full year at the Marine Hospital on the East coast, I gave morphine to badly injured people on several occasions and was then able to move them through similarly bad situations, with minimal discomfort. However, that wondrous, but addictive drug is not available to most civilians and I had none.

There were six of us to help Greg. With two of us dragging, "hopping" or carrying him, I placed Pat and Don up front trying to find the easiest route and signaling us with their flashlights. It saved us a lot of extra effort, misery and wasted time.

Every dwarf birch seemed to snag Greg's foot, relentlessly torturing the man.

Initially, everyone, especially one of the new guests, was on high alert for the rogue bear, but I told all that with so many of us making so much noise, there was little to fear from bears, so that worry should be suppressed. We needed to be concerned with Greg's comfort and getting back to the lodge as soon as possible. So we just slogged along as fast as conditions would permit. It was slow, but I kept telling all that we were making remarkably good time.

Encouragement, even if obviously overstated, usually helps.

We would move along for thirty minutes or so, then rest for five. Each stop, the second man bearing Greg would be relieved by another.

But I took no relief the entire trip. I knew everyone was already near their limit of physical endurance and figured if I did not take any less strenuous chore, the rest would be less inclined to suggest a slower pace. Adrenalin and spirit kicks in to allow people to push beyond their known limits and I was counting on this to keep us going. However, I did switch from right to left side which helped a lot. For most of the trip very few places allowed us to drag Greg. We had to either carry or "hop" him for nearly all of the four and a half mile (by GPS, which was more than double that on foot) journey. Several times he told me that he thought his arms were going to be torn off at the shoulder.

At every stop, I made Greg sip some water, warm soup, and eat a candy bar. He protested, but I wouldn't let him win on that. We needed to keep his blood sugar at as high a level as possible to combat shock and the damp, cold conditions. The soup was comforting, but the candy was more important.

The rain, mixed with snow kept coming as little squalls moved up from the south.

As the night wore on, Greg wanted longer rest periods. After several brief discussions on that topic, I just started fibbing to Greg, telling him that we had already been resting for half an hour, after only five minutes had passed. All the others knew that we had to move as fast as possible and none questioned my time keeping. Greg was no doubt suspicious, but he was in too much misery to really know or effectively resist.

Weather, as always, had us in its grip and this night it was cruel. Heavier snow began to fall, then morphed into a light, intermittent rain, but I had dressed lightly on purpose, knowing that I would not stop until we had Greg back in the lodge. The others were wearing heavy hunting coats and when Greg's coat got wet from being drug through the bogs, each man changed coats with Greg, trying to keep him from getting too chilled. When we did get back to the lodge, everyone's coat was soaked.

It seemed to take half of forever to get to Two Mile Ridge. In the overcast, it was plumb dark as we tried to ease Greg down through the rocks and gullies of the slope to the big cut bank next to Trail Creek. I could just make out the lone cottonwood that was nearby the best place to cross. The cut bank was slippery and muddy, so I went down first, facing back uphill, pulling when necessary on the tarp which bore Greg, with Jason and Lon stabilizing the upper end to keep it from going too fast or losing control.

We had about two hundred yards of deadfalls and brush to maneuver Greg through to the crossing. The river was waist deep there, but a barely discernible gravel bar allowed us to get across by walking diagonally to the main flow of the stream. By then, everyone was completely soaked with sweat and precipitation and with hip boots full of water, but our only thoughts were of Greg and getting him to the lodge.

Once across the river, everything seemed like duck soup. Before starting down with the others to find Greg and me, Pat had the presence of mind to park one Honda three wheeler and trailer as close to the river crossing as she could and we got Greg into the trailer to ride the last half mile.

Back to the Lodge

At the lodge, I fired up the oil stove, leaving Greg in the trailer until help caught up to us. With everyone there, we gently as possible, got Greg inside and onto a small cot.

I found Greg just before seven o'clock in the evening and we got back to the lodge after seven the next morning. That had been a miserable twelve hours, the like of which I hope none of us ever needs to repeat.

Days later I used a GPS to measure the distance - it was 4.5 miles, but, due to brush and terrane, we likely had been forced to travel twice or more that distance bringing Greg back.

Pat went upstairs to prepare some hot soup and sandwiches for everyone while I cut away Greg's hip boots and pants. I expected the left boot to be full of blood, but it showed very little. The leg was swollen and pale - the color alarmed me, but I felt confident that it could be saved. The bite on his thigh also looked nasty, but was of minor significance. I used "q-tips" and gauze, with physohex to debride the wounds, then covered them with clean gauze.

We helped him get out of his remaining wet cloths and into clean dry undies, shirt and pants. We helped him into his sleeping bag and placed mine on top of his in hopes of warming him faster. After being wet for several hours in the damp chill of that Arctic night, he was clearly hypothermic and I had to warm him up before flying to Kotzebue.

Greg had made me promise him that he could have one beer at the lodge, so I let him have one, but only after swallowing two bowls full of hot soup and more aspirin/codeine.

By nine that morning, we all laid down to rest, but I doubt that many actually slept. Pat stayed by Greg close to the stove and he seemed to doze off.

And again I thanked God for His wonderful help and directions in finding my friend and getting him back to the lodge.

At eleven that morning Pat had more hot food and sandwiches for everybody and all hands helped get Greg back into the trailer and then loaded into the super cub. We placed him with his feet pointed back and him facing backward with his back braced against the rear of the pilot seat.

Normally it takes an hour and a half to make the trip and we made the flight in about ninety-five minutes. As I approached, I called the FAA's Flight Service Station and asked that they call my son, Martin. I did not announce the situation, nor did I call for an ambulance. There was no need to make this situation a public one.

Soon I got a reply. The man on duty radioed me that Martin was hunting geese, but if I could use a hand, the Flight Service fellow, Jimmy, said he was going to take his lunch break and could come by with his truck. Many times the FSS boys would come by to see the big moose or caribou rack I had brought in, but this time was different.

I told my friend that I would appreciate some assistance. When Jimmy pulled up, he said that he heard something in my voice that told him I needed help.

We drove Greg to the United States Public Health Service hospital emergency entrance and asked for a stretcher.

The lady physician was new to the area and had not a lot of experience in this sort of injury, but she was very cooperative and easy to deal with. When she removed the gauze bandage from his thigh, she gasped at the injury, exclaiming that it was already infected.

I told her, "No, that's just subcutaneous fat, but we need to get this man sedated as soon as possible, as he has endured a very rough twenty-four hours with compound, complex fractures of his tibia and fibula."

She asked me who I was and one of the two attending nurses said "That's Doctor Jacobson."

"I'm not a real Doctor," I replied.

"That doesn't matter, scrub in!" she told me.

Immediately I asked the nurse to bring a power of attorney form for Greg to sign, in case I needed to make any decisions for him. I also asked that she lay out everything from his pockets and make an inventory list. I had not thought of these things before and still don't know how they came to mind at the time, but I am glad they floated to the top of my stressed grey matter when they did. Then I remembered that I had made an urgent prayer that I "be granted the right reactions and led to the best decisions" - that must have been it!

Greg had over twenty-two hundred dollars in one pocket, which surprised everyone, and it did not get misplaced during his treatment.

The Doc put Greg under with an intravenous sedative and cut away the ankle bandage, then the technician took an x-ray. The radiograph revealed some wires and a staple in his leg, that had been placed in his leg after previous injuries. I told the nurse to make a note for me to take a box of staples up to camp to replace the one we pulled off the fence for Greg's leg.

The Doctor gasped, then glared at me, questioning? I told her it was my attempt to lighten the mood. Greg had been through a hellish time, but now he was going to be fine.

The Doc used her scissors to cut away Greg's shorts and when she pulled them loose, she let out a loud gasp. Lying there, innocent, unconscious, and unable to defend himself, Greg displayed a whanger that would be the envy of a pony, ... or a horse.

Both nurses giggled. It was a bit of comic or maybe phallic relief.

The real doctor and I agreed that we should attempt to re-set, then stabilize the leg fractures before transporting him to an orthopedic surgeon.

We got Greg's leg straightened up as much as we could, took a new x-ray and cast it with plaster. As this was being done, I think nearly every female employee of the hospital stopped by. Word had spread and it seemed each one wanted to have a gander at Greg's extraordinary anatomical feature that had been revealed in the emergency room!

I suggested that someone get a sheet or towel to cover poor Greg's nether region. After all, I was acting as his designated advocate. On the other hand, maybe I should have just set up a nurse to collect admission fees to help with his medical bills?

Someone mentioned a Medevac flight and I asked about the comment. The Doc had ordered a plane. I told her to cancel the order. After what Greg had endured, a First Class flight to Anchorage and beyond would be a pure delight and there was no reason to waste fifty thousand dollars of anybody's money on an emergency Medevac. The real emergency had taken place the day before and it was long since over.

Then I heard an ambulance had been scheduled to meet Greg when he got to Anchorage and transport him to Providence Hospital. I told them to cancel that, too and for everyone to clear any other arrangements with me before making them. I was going to ship Greg all the way to Idaho Falls where his own physician, family, and friends could care for him.

Sometimes procedures, including Medivac and ambulance services are so cut and dried that no one questions the necessity of any of those costly measures, especially in situations where the government or an insurance company is paying all the bills. It's just follow the "cook book" and proceed with head up and locked. This drives the cost of health care up. And neither Greg nor I carried medical insurance. We were lucky both services were cancelled in time.

My friend, Jimmy, from FAA came by the hospital with a First Class upgrade for Greg, but the Alaska Airlines lady station manager told me that he didn't need it, this one was "on the house" and his trip all the way to Idaho Falls would be as a First Class passenger at no extra fee, compliments of Alaska Airlines.

When the sedative wore off, Greg asked for a hamburger, so I went to get one and returned. Some of my grandkids had heard of the accident and were standing in Greg's room. My daughter, Sandy and some of the little kids came in and hugged me. Sandy said the rumor mill was reporting that it was me who had been badly mauled.

I wrote down the names of everyone that had helped with Greg and told them that I would be contacting them soon.

The Alaska Airlines jet was due at six-thirty that evening, but it was delayed for three hours. Greg sat in a wheel chair at the terminal and the time dragged by very slowly. Luckily the powerful analgesics from the hospital muted his pain and he had oral meds in sufficient supply to get him home in relative comfort. Fatigue was setting in on me. I was offered a place to sit down and gratefully took the seat.

My son-in-law, Alan, worked for Alaska Airlines and I asked him to accompany Greg to Anchorage. I called my friend, Jim Cann, to meet the plane and help Greg get on the most direct jet flight to Idaho Falls.

Before the departing jet's contrails had dissipated, I was at my daughter Sandy's house. I'd not slept for 40 hours, so one beer and a snack put me into a deep slumber on her couch.

Aftermath

Early the next morning, I called home and told the awful tale to my wife, Teresa. She had already been informed by Sandy and she told me that my six year old daughter, Bess was anxiously waiting to talk with me.

"Papa, you have to go find and kill that mean bear before it hurts anyone else, but, Papa, take LOTS of guns", Bess instructed me in her most serious tone. She knew our family rules - Duty First, Safety Always.

It's funny how things like that stick in one's memory.

Before noon I landed my super cub at Trail Creek. After filling everyone in on Greg's situation, I took Don and returned to the site of the attack in hopes of finding the bear's dead carcass. Watching carefully for ravens, we saw nothing. The rain and snow showers had removed what little chance of a blood trail might have been. We spent eight hours scouring the area for the bear, but found no sign whatsoever of the Grizzly. When we returned shortly after dark, we were both just plain worn out.

It was humbling to think of how everyone had performed in the emergency. Jason, with a pulled groin muscle, Pat with a bad ankle, Don, at age sixty-five, walking well over twenty miles that day and probably ten miles the next day, Dick (also affectionately know as Dr. Brittanica because he had a wealth of useful information on most everything), and Lon all persevering in adverse weather and tough conditions. No one gave up or complained.

Truly, these folks all had risen to the occasion.

After the fruitless search for the wounded bear I ate a little, then slept soundly for ten hours. When I awoke, I was sore all over. My right shoulder was especially bothersome. Most of the soreness was gone in a day or so, and after a couple of months the shoulder discomfort became less miserable, but it is still with me as I write this seventeen years later. I never can sleep on my right side, as the pain soon kicks in. That sure messes up my hair on the left side!

In late September, the night before I departed Kotzebue to return to Kodiak, I bought flowers for the Doctor and nurses and invited everyone who had helped with Greg to a steak dinner at the Bayside Restaurant. All had given their best efforts in Greg's behalf, and this was the least, I needed to do for them. The doctor was on call at the hospital so I took her steak and flowers to her, along with my heartfelt thanks.

Since 2001, I have kept a reliable Satellite Telephone at the lodge, but having one during Greg's incident would not have helped. We got him out as soon as it could have been done. I've long debated carrying small hand held radios for safety, but such communications are illegal for hunting pursuits in Alaska and I'm convinced that having them would lead to misuse. Had we been using them, I might have found Greg sooner, but not that much quicker.

The Next Guest Hunter

Three days after Greg's mauling, about six inches of new snow had accumulated when the chartered Cessna 185 came to take the guests back to Kotzebue. Caribou had not been seen by any of us in the valley for several days, but as the charter landed, a herd of several hundred was grazing about a quarter of a mile north of the lodge. Murphy plays cruel tricks, sometimes. I asked the charter pilot be sure to fly the guys over the caribou, to see for themselves, rather than just hear it from me.

Only one hunter, a plumber named Bob, a good friend, who I call Plumb Bob, made it for the next booking.

Plumb Bob's wife, who I call Tundra Plumb, (but she's really a peach of a gal) had made his flight reservations, but after hearing of Greg's mauling, she had reservations about Bob coming to hunt at all. Bob came anyway.

Plumb Bob with a decent bull in September 2000.

Bob and I watched the caribou all day without molesting them. Alaska law forbids shooting most big game animals until after three o'clock in the morning of the day following a flight.

The next morning, needless to say, we were up well before daylight, having coffee and getting ready, when at first light, a large black wolf walked by the lodge at about 200 yards. We eased out the door and walked north through the willows to see the same wolf standing on a gravel bar between us and a large band of caribou. The wolf was about ninety yards away and looking right at us.

I whispered to Plumb Bob to shoot, he was kneeling, and I kept expecting to hear the report of his rifle. After a minute, the wolf turned and began to run away. Then Bob opened up and shot several times, but did not connect. I asked him why he didn't take the easy, standing shot. He explained that he was an Arkansas turkey hunter and you don't shoot them until they turn broadside, allowing the pellets to penetrate the feathers more effectively.

My reply was that we should check out the caribou and talk turkey later.

Plumb Bob and the second aggressive Grizzly in seven days.

Plumb Bob took a nice bull and for the next several days, the caribou kept coming steadily down Trail Creek.

One week to the day after Greg's mauling, Plumb Bob and I were sitting on a small rise, well below the ridge line to avoid being seen, as we watched several hundred caribou feeding in the open ground below us. East Bowl Creek with it's line of willows ran along the north side of the open area.

A Toklat colored Grizzly appeared at the far end of the brush laced flat and began feeding on soap berries as he moved toward us. Caribou kept a respectable distance between themselves and the ambling Grizzly, but they watched the bear and did not run far away.

At well over three hundred and fifty yards the bear seemed to focus on us. We were very discretely situated ... not lumps on the bear's horizon and we were wearing camouflage jackets. The bear stood on it's hind legs, then dropped to all fours, running directly at us. Somehow, this supposedly myopic bruin had seen us! It was a smaller bear than I normally allow a guest to shoot.

2000, Greg Fischer's Mauling

Protein enriched spaghetti from the bear's stomach.

As the oncoming bear closed the distance, Plumb Bob, who was legal for a bear, asked if he should shoot. I said, no, but put one up the spout, just in case. I jacked a round into my chamber, too.

When the bear was fifty yards from us, I stood up, waved my hat and yelled, "Get out of here, you idiot !"

The rushing Grizzly was not phased, he just kept on loping to us, so at 25 yards I told Plumb Bob to shoot. His bullet struck the bear near the center of its chest, but the bear did not slow down. I hollered to shoot him again. The second chest shot slowed the beast and turned it to the right. A third shot broke the bear's spine at the withers and the animal crumpled.

This six year old boar was not large, squaring a bit over six feet, but it was beautifully marked with a dark brown line running along the spine, chocolate legs and feet, but otherwise blonde - a Toklat - like so many we find at Trail Creek. It was not fat. The stomach was stuffed full of soap berries and the gut was full of round worms.

Plumb Bob and his meat moose.

How the bear was able to see us still puzzles me. Why it decided to rush us is an enigma, as well. More than fifteen years later, I still have no explanation. Two Grizzly attacks in one week is unusual. Such visual acuity is even less common.

Plumb Bob had harvested several bull moose with me, including one large bull, so he was primarily concerned with getting some moose meat. As a resident of Alaska he could shoot a moose with less than a fifty-five inch antler spread. From the main window of the lodge we spotted a legal bull moose one morning down in the direction of the route we had used to retrieve Greg. We made out way quickly, then set up to glass the patch of willows where we'd last seen the moose. After forty minutes I saw the flash of a horn as the moose moved in its bed. Bob and I got close and as he was about to shoot, an aircraft with Federal Government markings flew over and landed on my strip. We watched as two men walked to the lodge.

Well, we were hunting and had no obligation to go greet uninvited guests, so I told Bob to go ahead and dispatch the meat moose. Which he handily did.

Before we walked the thirty yards or so to the moose, we saw the two men come running from the lodge to their airplane, get in and take off. They probably heard Bob's shot, but I wondered why they acted so spooky. I hoped they did not think anyone was shooting at them.

So now we had a bunch of meat to get to Kotzebue. I would take in one maximum load of meat, then come get Bob for the rest and the bear skin and caribou rack. In just a few days we'd gone from a lack of prey species to plenty and from snow cover to bare ground. Such is September in the Arctic I've come to know and love.

Plumb Bob headed back to Kodiak with his meat and trophies and I returned to the lodge to close up and quietly think over and write down the events of the past two weeks.

Reflections

In analyzing the incident with Greg Fischer, I have some thoughts. I believe the big bear was sleeping soundly when it heard Don nearby, then hearing Greg shout, it launched into automatic, reflex action and attacked Greg. I believe that, had it not been for Don's shooting, the bear's next act would have been to disembowel Greg, killing him. We confirmed in 2003 that the bear was an old boar. Greg's two shots had connected, and that, too, may have been a factor in causing the bear to discontinue it's attack.

Dick, who with me, saw the sow and cub come running out of a different willow patch, posed his theory that the sow had mauled Greg, but Don did not see a second bear, and we conclusively discounted that a few years later, after examining the bear. It was a large boar that had indeed, done the deed.

Greg's Recovery

Greg's healing was slow and agonizing with a long hospital stay. He developed a dangerous infection which took weeks to clear up. At one point his physician prescribed that he take rabies shots, but I urged him not to put himself through that painful regime and Greg declined the vaccination series. No way that bear was rabid.

He and his physician seriously contemplated amputation of his left leg, but things began to improve, albeit slowly.

Several surgeries later, a ticonium rod was placed in his left tibia, but the leg healed up a bit crooked and was shorter than the other side. Even so, he's far better off than he would be as an amputee.

Facing huge medical bills, Greg took his contracted deer and elk hunters into the Wyoming mountains in October and November, that same year, but his horse fell and rolled on his as yet unhealed leg, further delaying and complicating the healing.

That fall, I spoke by telephone frequently with Greg and he said he'd like to get drawn for a Grizzly permit, so I made application for him. He assured me that he was not angry with the bear, he just wanted to hunt one.

Greg Fisher's Return to Trail Creek

No luck came for Greg in the 2001 or 2002 drawings, but in 2003 he got drawn for a Grizzly Permit. Greg and I kept in frequent telephone contact.

On August 30, our three incoming guests, including Greg, Plumb Bob and Grant, arrived on a Cessna 206 charter which took my daughters and grandsons back to Kotzebue on the return leg. I brought the cub up later with a load of groceries. I saw no Caribou within twenty miles of the lodge that evening.

In the early light of August 31, we glassed over two hundred caribou on the northwest alluvial fan and that afternoon our guests took two bulls after allowing a considerable number of animals to pass by, on their annual southerly migration.

On September 1, Gregg and I started up the creek, but found a big bull caribou in a band of about twenty-five animals just a quarter of a mile from the cabin. After a short stalk, he shot the big one which turned out to be the best of the season for us - and number three in the statewide competition.

PlumbBob, Barry and Grant each took a good bull that afternoon, a mile down creek from the lodge.

On September 2, I went to Kotzebue to pick up another guest, Barry. Caribou kept coming down Trail Creek, but none were taken that day. On September 3, Barry took a nice bull while Bob and Rob, my assistant guide, pursued one up into West Bowl Canyon which Bob took. That was a challenging stalk and a laborious pack out of that brush choked canyon. Next to Greg's bull, it was the best caribou so far that season for us.

Everybody was seeing and taking game and it was a very happy camp.

On the night of September 4, a Grizzly left its large footprint near the meat rack and had removed two caribou quarters. At first light the following morning I saw a blondish bear enter a willow patch on the southeast side of Trail Creek. It was a blustery, cold day, but we all posted on the East Moguls, taking turns watching for the bear. I told everyone that I was sure the bear was holed up in the willow patch I saw it enter, and I expected it to get up eventually to relieve itself, at which time we might spot it.

Greg Fischer and his Statewide #3 Caribou, 2003.

Bears do not mess their own nest. But when it had not showed itself by five o'clock, leaving Plumb Bob to keep an eye on the area, I returned to the lodge with Greg to finish up the turkey dinner. Shortly, Plumb Bob came running back to say that he saw the bear emerge about fifteen minutes after Gregg and I left the hill. Greg, Rob Coyle, my Assistant guide and I intercepted the bear on its way toward the lodge and Gregg shot it. This boar measured about seven and a half feet square and I've never seen a prettier Grizzly. It was creamy white with chocolate legs and a dark stripe running down the middle of it's back - another "Toklat" Grizzly. It was very well furred - even in the groin area. Gregg was elated - and, it appeared that we had the camp bear, on Gregg's birthday. This was a far nicer gift than the one he received three years before !

However, the following morning we awoke to find the "A" frame meat rack completely demolished. And a bear had dragged it about five yards south into the blueberry bog. The danged bruin had chewed every piece of meat on the rack, at least partially swallowing some of each piece of this smorgasbord. I rebuilt the rack and rehung the ragged chunks of meat, then rigged a trip line connected to a bell inside the top floor of the lodge. I also loaded the twelve gage shotgun with buckshot and slugs, leaving a

Plumb Bob, Greg, Barry, and Grant with caribou racks.

round in the chamber for everyone to carry to the outhouse - just in case. But the shotgun was a pump and not everyone is familiar with such guns, so I loaded up the lever action thirty-thirty with the outside hammer. Every guy knows how to work a John Wayne carbine, so that would be the safest piece for the boys to carry to the outhouse.

On night three of the camp bear, September 6, we waited, but the bear did not return. Caribou continued their passage down Trail Creek and we saw a wolverine, a porcupine and a couple moose, as well as many sheep ... all pretty common sightings for that time of the year.

The night of September 7 - night four of the camp bear - we went to bed about 10:30pm, with Plumb Bob sleeping on the couch near the window on the top floor, close to the trip line bell, with his rifle close at hand. At ten minutes to eleven, the bell tinkled. Before I could join them, Plumb Bob and Rob Coyle slid the window open to see the big Grizzly below that same window, just next to the parked Honda three-wheelers. Bob shot the bear in the top of the withers and it charged off into the darkness. He said he was sure it was a good hit.

PlumbBob wanted to pursue the bear, right then, but I told him we'd wait for daylight. There was no way I was going to search for any wounded grizzly in heavy cover and full darkness.

At first light we saw the bear lying about fifteen feet from where it had been shot. It was lying behind a willow bush in the yard of the lodge, stone dead. Bob's bullet had pierced the top of the heart, destroying both the atria and shutting off blood blow immediately.

As we posed the bear for the pictures, Greg said he recognized that face. He said it was the bear that mauled him, three years before!

It was a surprise to us all to see that it's left front leg had not been in use for some time, with marks on the back of the claws from being dragged along, rather than used normally. After skinning, an old injury to the right hip was also apparent. Gregg reminded me that he told me his first shot at the charging Grizzly, three years before, had been a bit high - which explained the healed hip wound - and his second shot at point blank range had been into the bear's chest. It seems that second shot was a bit to the left of center. Gregg was certain that this Grizzly was the one that attacked him in 2000. I tried my best to find a bullet at each injury site, but I was unable to locate any lead fragments.

Greg's Grizzly was as pretty as they get!

I measured the distance between the bear's maxillary canines - the bite radius - and they matched what I recorded after the mauling.

It all seemed to make sense, though, and I believe that was the bear that mauled Gregg.

So we lost quite a bit of caribou meat, but that was insignificant compared to Gregg's loss in 2000 and compared to what might have been with this old, crippled "man-eater" Grizzly.

This big Grizzly placed number three in the statewide Alaska Professional Hunters' /Safari Club International Big Three Competition for 2003.

*In 2005, Greg's story was written up in a book, BEAR ATTACKS OF THE CENTURY, by Larry Mueller and Marguerite Reiss.

Greg showing how the other bear bit him in 2000.

But I figured such an event demanded a complete narrative from one who was there for all but the initial attack.

Back for a Ram

Greg's mobility and agility was still compromised but he was beginning to get around pretty well. After ten years of closure to sport hunting, 2004 was to be the first year since 1994 that anything but local subsistence hunting of Dall rams was allowed in northwest Alaska. I suggested that Greg have me apply for a Dall Ram permit for him. He agreed, reminding me that I still had to come to Wyoming for an elk and mountain mule Deer hunt. I said that would just have to happen when it happens - when both our schedules meshed and minimized cost to each of us.

Greg joined my grandson, Spencer, and I on August 20. Trail Creek was overrun with caribou. Hundreds of the tundra deer were coming down the valley every day. We'd glassed a good Dall ram on Middle Mountain, to the East and another dandy ram in West Bowl. I left the other hunter, Milton and Milton's wife with Spencer to look over caribou while Greg and I went for the west side ram.

We got high and followed the ridge line, expecting to see the ram below us, but finding nothing we continued deep along the high ridges into the range. I had taken Alaska's only U.S. Congressman Don Young up the same route in 1984, returning with an old, heavily broomed ram.

After eight hours on the mountain we had not seen a single ram, so we turned around and headed for camp. Passing across a shale slide I looked back and saw the big ram lying

The underside of Greg's bear was dark in color.

below and within 150 yards of us. We had been fully exposed to this sheep for nearly five minutes, but it apparently was sound asleep. No glassing was necessary to ascertain that this was the right ram. Greg shot it as I filmed the episode making that evening hunt about as good as it could possibly be.

Dall ram testicles are normally very large, but the left testis on this old ram was enlarged beyond any that I had ever seen. I removed the scrotum and both testes for delivery to the National Park Service biologist.

The Park Service and Arctic Institute examinations revealed that this animal carried brucellosis. It was the only recorded case of that disease in wild Dall sheep.

With Greg's leg still troublesome, I packed the entire ram out - meat, head and cape, but that has often been the case on sheep hunts over the previous thirty-three years.

As I set about caping the animal, I noticed that it's right eye was opaque - it was obviously blind on that side. Had it not been for that, our careless exposure above him would have likely resulted in the animal running off

Grant and PlumbBob with the grizzly that mauled Greg in 2000.

without Greg ever getting a shot. Perhaps we would never have even seen that ram.

When we reached the main valley I saw Spencer and Milt in a stalking mode, so I dropped my heavy pack and joined them. Milton took a dandy big bull caribou, which we gutted and covered with willow branches to pick up the next day.

Things just don't get much better than that!

With his trophy taken early in his booking, Milton and his wife chartered back to Kotzebue to enable them to visit McKinley Park, giving Spencer, Greg and I several days to look over caribou. Spencer shot three good bulls for meat to take home and we had daily entertainment provided by the many big game animals passing down the valley.

As we were loading Greg's gear and trophy into the cub to depart, I spotted an outstanding caribou near the site of Milton's kill. I fussed with Greg to take it, he wanted to leave it for someone else, but I prevailed - explaining to him that unlike deer, caribou are always on the move and

ALASKA BEARS   Stirred and Shaken

Greg and the first Alaska Game Management Unit 23 sport harvested ram in ten years.

Our guest, Milton, Spencer and bull caribou.

Spencer and Greg with the 2004, #2 Caribou.

that huge bull would be gone soon. Finally I convinced Greg to shoot it. This great bull placed number two in the Safari Club International/ Alaska Professional Hunters' Association annual Big Three Competition for the year.

Greg's first trip to Trail Creek ended in a disaster, but he never gave up, he hung in there, and his next two trips were about as good as they get.

A Weekend in Kodiak

The extraordinarily cold, windy weather, accompanied by record snow cover made the winter of 2011/2012 fatally hard on a large percentage of the Kodiak Archipelago's Sitka Blacktail deer. I was expecting a late onset of the next winter, but in mid October I realized I was mistaken. Accompanied by my young friend, Joey Coyle, the sixteen year old son of a close friend, we took the mail plane to the south end of Kodiak on October 18, 2012, expecting to spend the next week in pursuit of deer for winter meat. Joey, the mail plane pilot, and I were surprised to find the lake of our intended campsite frozen. Having hunted the area previously, I figured it would be usable by float planes until sometime in early November. So much for my weather prognostications.

Never subject to the extreme highs and lows of snowshoe hare populations as occur on mainland Alaska, the snowshoe hares remain pretty steady on Kodiak. I was thankful for that and, due to the lack of deer in our freezer, I intended to supplement our diet with more bunnies than usual.

Deer were reported to be scarce all over the region, but I was seeing more in my yard that fall than ever before. As I live outside the city limits, with dense timber abutting my back yard, I contemplated shooting a breathing biomass of venison out the window, given an appropriate opportunity, but one never came. I probably wouldn't have done it, anyway.

Each morning I saw fresh deer tracks in the moss that had displaced the grass in the back yard and I checked the yard faithfully each dawn.

One Saturday morning I peered out the window. As the sun was struggling to rise, a beautiful frosting was being added to every exposed surface. I watched the frost forming, as often happens just before dawn. This heavy white coating would facilitate detection of new tracks, all of which would have to be as fresh as the morning.

After scrutinizing the shadows with special attention to the brush along the property line, I went to the computer to peruse the news. As is often the case, a couple of news stories held my attention and after digesting them I looked out the window -thinking and hoping for deer.

No sign of anything with hair, fur or feathers was to be seen, but glaring back at me was a set of fresh bear tracks smashed through the new frost. The large beast had walked past our front door, literally just beneath my nose, skirted around the sandbox and strolled across the yard, passing mere inches from our kids' trampoline before entering the recently leafless salmonberry brush that borders the heavy timber. And I, temporarily absorbed by political trivia, had missed the action and photo opportunity.

The local radio station had been broadcasting reports of several bears - a dozen or so - engaged in cohabitation with the human community, and well within the city limits. The announcements were voiced as mild, perfunctory warnings, along with assurances that the giant bears were not troublesome. After all, we are often reminded, the bears occupied this area long before humans came and they are just "doing their thing", which this time of year means they are gorging their alimentary canals with anything and everything they can cram down their throats, in anticipation of a long, cold, hungry, winter. They were indiscriminately feasting now in preparation for their upcoming, slumbering fast.

Local officials voiced their heartfelt pride at the tolerance and, might we say, forbearance, of Kodiak citizens, who, up to that point, had not killed a single one of our urban bruins this season. Well ... so far.

Stifling my self rebuke in favor of salvaging what I could from the missed opportunity for some great, close-up photographs of our lawn guest, I grabbed my packet of video and still cameras and eased out the door, carefully eyeballing our pickup parked nearby, in case the bear might have decided it was a nice place to lie, or lean against.

Satisfied that the area was apparently bear free, if not the least unbearable, I proceeded the short distance to the tracks.

After again quickly double checking that the bruin was not loitering nearby, I took out my camera and preserved the evidence on the microchip. The boot next to the track is size 12, and insulated, to give one a

My insulated boot is size 12. Note the bear's long stride.

comparison. It wasn't a huge bear by Kodiak standards - maybe an eight and a half footer, but it left some impressive foot prints.

So much for that. I went back to the news paper, trying to make sense of some of the ongoing political imponderables, deplorables, and just plain craziness. Then I struck off for the grocery store and a hot, fresh jalapeno bagel.

The next morning - that would be Sunday - I again turned my attention to the internet version of the newspaper. But this time, I interrupted my consumption of published gossip, which often masquerades as news, every minute or so, to check for deer or our other recent visitor. But with no success. Only a pair of magpies hopped about, apparently expecting a bug to emerge from the frost covered lawn - or an iceworm, maybe?

Then my telephone rang. It was my friend, Doug Pederson who asked what I planned to do that day.

I responded that I had nothing special in mind, but since he called, I expected to be involved in some interesting project which he was about to describe to me.

"Well, last night I had to shoot a bear that was in my henhouse, killing my chickens. I duct taped a flashlight to my .338 which I hadn't shot for twenty-five years, and yelled at the bear to get out of there. When it came toward me I shot it in the head," Doug reported. Doug had given the bear a verbal warning to cease and desist its depredations, but the bear ignored it, to its peril.

"Could you use some help getting it out & skinning it?", I suggested.

"Yeah, if you're not too busy," Doug replied.

"Never too busy for such an enterprise with a friend like you," I assured him.

Bear season was set to open only four days later, but dispatching a marauding *Ursus arctos* in defense of life or property is legal, and often immediately necessary. One catch is, the shooter is responsible for skinning the thing and surrendering the hide and skull to the Alaska Department of Fish and Game. That can be a truly onerous burden if the killing takes place in the deep bush, especially if it requires packing the hide out (often for several miles) to a place from which it can be transported by boat, land vehicle, or aircraft to the authorities.

Anyone care for a forkfull of bear?

The term "packing through the alders" brings thoughtful reminiscences for those who have done so, and imaginable nightmares for those who who have yet to experience the chore.

But this was not the case with the chicken molester and hen killer.

Doug suggested that we begin around one o'clock in the afternoon, so after church I gathered up my rain gear, knife and sharpener and drove the mile or so to Doug's place.

He had already winched the carcass out of the chicken yard and had it hanging near his front door from a large fork lift when I arrived.

The next act was to maneuver the rig down the hill to Doug's junk yard. Doug has one of the best junkyards I have ever seen. It's more interesting than most museums I have visited, and a heckuva lot more useful. Just that past summer I needed an axel for my boat trailer and inquired of my friend. He said he thought he still had the one I gave him a few years ago ... best yet, he knew where it was! Most everybody in these parts hangs onto anything that might be useful - you never know when you or a buddy might need it. However, it's uncommon to find such parts right off the bat. It might take as much time to dig one up as it would to order one from a retail supply store in the lower forty-eight. It's cheaper though, if you've the time. But I digress.

Once we had the bear hanging in the junk yard I realized that in my forty-five years of skinning various species and sizes of bears, in most every position I found them, I have never done one that was hanging. I had to ask Doug to lower it to the ground to give me access to make the initial square cuts to aid a taxidermist in making a nice rug mount. This brownie was well furred, with some rubbed spots, and it would likely be auctioned off by the Alaska Department of Fish and Game. The buyer would probably have a rug made.

Once we had the legs pretty well skinned and the feet knuckled out, hoisting the carcass back up made the rest of the job easy. Actually, it was the easiest job of skinning a bear in which I ever participated.

This bear did not smell fishy or bad at all. We eat sweet smelling mountain Grizzlies in the Arctic - they taste a lot like beef. When I first came on the scene in Kodiak in 1967, local people hunted the great bears for meat. Once deer became abundant, bear meat lost its preference as mainstay in the diet of most folks here. But we salvaged the four quarters and they were given to some old timers who knew and appreciated bear meat. I was thinking that maybe I should have kept some - what with the deer population so low and all.

The next day another bear was shot in another nearby henhouse, but the radio reported that the wounded bruin ran off. I wondered if it might be wadded up underneath some unsuspecting person's porch.

Bear season opened the following Thursday and a guide friend, Frank Bishop took a guest to Bill Burton's buffalo ranch and shot a huge boar over a cow the thing had killed a few hundred yards from the house. That mega bear squared over ten feet eight inches and had a skull of over 30 inches, which after drying will probably earn it ninth place in the record book.

Ready to peel the beast, with Doug's grand nephew supervising.

With no snow at lower elevations, the bears remained active in Kodiak town and the nearby residential areas. On November 5, I noticed that our dumpster had been moved from its normal location about a half mile from our house. Officials figured it might attract the big carnivores and moving the garbage bins would take them elsewhere, I suppose. Transfer the problems next door and to someone else was the idea, it seems. Oh well, government goofiness begins in one's home town.

My friend and the truly giant bear. PHOTO BY FRANK BISHOP

In my fifty years of guiding in Alaska I have had dozens of encounters with "cabin bears". Rarely do such wild animals make a single visit. Once intrigued - or worse yet, entertained - with some form of food or diversion, most bruins make repeated rendezvous, becoming more bold with each encounter. Town bears are not much different from remote cabin bears in my estimation. Eventually, most cabin bears wind up being killed by the cabin's human owners.

My feeling is that we have refuges for bears and other wildlife where human activities are restricted. In some such refuges firearms may not be carried under any circumstances. I believe that human residential areas should be reserved for people, their pets, and their domestic animals and therefore, dangerous wildlife such as bears and rattlesnakes should be removed (i.e., killed) when they frequent those areas. Unfortunately, it seems inevitable to me that some person, most likely a child, will be attacked by an urbanized "cabin bear". Often little pet dogs get boogered by a bear and run back to their owners, bringing the agitated bear with them. I hope I am wrong regarding that dismal forecast.

It's just as well that we have no rattlesnakes on Kodiak Island.

A Weekend in Kodiak

Three brown bears visiting the Kodiak post office. THIS PHOTO WAS POSTED ON FACEBOOK, PHOTOGRAPHER UNKNOWN

Dumpsters attract bears.

It Takes a Girl to Kill a Grizzly

In 1982, my Dad came up to help with hunters and enjoy the far north with the family. There was still a little pecking around to do with interior work, such as trim and painting on the lodge and sauna, but mostly we were just going with the flow, with no major projects nagging at us other than taking care of our guest hunters. The guests had taken their trophies and now were focused on doing some fishing in the creek and a little ptarmigan hunting.

On one of my extra trips to town for supplies, I brought Dave Johnson, the Alaska Department of Fish and Game biologist from Kotzebue up for a few days of field work, observations, and biological sampling.

Weather had been pleasant with no major storms, all types of berries, blue, cran, crow, and soap berries, were abundant. Fish were stacked up like cord wood in the streams, caribou were coming down the valley, with new herds appearing each day. Every day we saw dozens of Dall sheep from the windows. We were in a hunter's paradise.

We were enjoying one of those all too brief brief, and sometimes nonexistent, late summer windows of heavenly conditions at Trail Creek.

One of our guests was an Alaskan resident who, after tasting the meat, wanted to take an extra caribou. I had something going on at the airplane - I think I was replacing the inner tube from the tail wheel, when a mob of caribou came down the eastern side hill next to the lodge.

Pop, my sister Pat, and the hunter went up to intercept the caribou and one fat bull went down. Pat and the hunter went back to get the pack boards as Pop gutted and began to quarter the 'bou when a medium sized grizzly came up over a little knoll and ran right to Pop. My Dad had his head down cutting off a hind leg when he looked up to see the bear alarmingly close and coming fast. He let out a whoop, which slowed the bear down.

As my Dad shouldered his rifle, the bear walked slowly toward him, grabbed the nearby caribou skin, then turned and dragging the bloody skin, ran up the hill. My labrador, Max, had gone to the cabin with Pat and the hunter, or he would have interceded, no doubt.

I never saw any of it, but heard it very thoroughly described by each of the three participants over supper.

Cabin bear encounters, though stimulating, are not desirable entertainment.

Such Grizzlies invariably get bolder and bolder and eventually, most get killed for their indiscretions or destructive actions, often by other bears. This adult boar kept hanging around on the east slopes of Trail Creek. We were seeing him on a daily basis.

Our outdoor biffy is about sixty yards from the lodge and everyone is instructed to always carry an adequate firearm on their visits to the throne. After years of experience and pondering the possibilities, I decided that carrying their own rifle was the most safe and effective way to go. An alternative would be a short barreled pump shotgun that I kept in camp, but a lever action 30:30 was probably more dependable and much safer in a tight squeeze, especially for someone not accustomed to the shotgun. Those not intimately experienced with the pump gun might be more apt to jam the action or accidentally discharge the weapon. But everybody knows how to lever a round into a John Wayne style of rifle. The outside hammer is an important safety feature as well. The Winchester Model 94 is ideal for this purpose.

Early one evening I went to the dip water creek with two empty buckets. Water levels had dropped and I had dug a deeper hole a little further than usual from the building. As I turned to go back to the lodge after dipping the second bucket full of the clear, cold water I heard splashing coming from up the creek. The source of the disturbance was that same nuisance bear coming, splashing his way, full tilt down the creek at me.

Unarmed, I ran for the lodge, buckets in hand. About midway to the door it dawned on me that I should drop the buckets and I did so, adding a bit of speed to my flight. I was hollering, "BEAR, BEAR, to alert anyone else that might have gone out of the building.

All our building doors open to the outside. I hung them that way to prevent a bear from slamming into the door, dislodging it and getting inside, which would be more likely if the doors opened to the inside.

I got in and pulled the door closed.

Within a second, or maybe three, the bear hit the door hard. Thank God we had taken this into account when we built the place or that bear would have been on me before I could get up the stairs.

The bear slammed into the steel door two more times, then went to the freshly spilled buckets and slapped them both around, sending them clattering into the willow bushes, as we looked on from the window.

After a cursory snoop around the yard, the bruin looked up at us before sullenly ambling off toward the biffy. Clearly this bear thought he was dominant and wanted us to know that he was the meanest, toughest fellow in the valley.

We stayed inside the lodge until the bear showed up on the eastern foothills. I was thankful that he had not decided to give the airplane a beating. If I had seen that developing, tag or not, I would have shot him for sure.

That bear had outlived his welcome and my level of tolerance. He had to go.

No one at the lodge was legal to take a grizzly, so I decided to go to Kotzebue and bring either my son, Martin, or daughter, Sandy, up to dispatch the cabin bear.

I told Pop that it would be a good idea if my sister harvested a nice fat caribou bull the next day and hang it on the meat pole. Hopefully the bear would not get at the meat before I returned with a shooter. My dog, Max, a black labrador retriever, should accompany anyone who went to get the caribou, as the dog would be extra insurance that a bear would not get too close again without being seen. And the caribou should be attended to by at least two people. Another close encounter as my Dad had recently experienced might not end up so benign. This malevolent grizzly had gotten away with some outrageous behavior and would become more self assertive and unpleasant as time passed.

Martin was working at the grocery store and the manager told me that with the last supply barge arriving soon, it would be very unhandy for him to be gone for a few days, so I called the school and told them that my daughter had to go to camp to protect us from a marauding bear. The principal got a kick out of that and asked that he be told the story when I brought Sandy back to school. He emphasized that he had never before been asked to excuse any student, let alone a girl, for such a purpose. I promised to give him all the details when the deed was done.

As we were leaving the house, I grabbed a couple of small brass bells that we used on the dog harnesses during Christmas mushing events around town. They would have a new purpose.

Sandy was happy to be called to duty - and away from school - and I landed at the lodge with her well before dark that same day. I placed some small pebbles in empty cans and strung them on a wire on the meat pole. We had some fresh Caribou meat, taken by Pat that same day, which hung on the meat pole, about twenty yards from the lodge. I ran a nylon line from the fresh meat up to the nearest window of the lodge and tied the little bells to it. That would serve as our jury-rigged burglar alarm.

But Murphy was apparently overseeing the operation, as no one had seen the bear that day. It figured. Murphy seldom naps, I've noticed.

We had a great supper of caribou back strap, rice and salad, with fresh crow berry pie for desert. We turned off the lanterns and waited quietly, but soon everyone had drifted off to sleep.

Sandy and I each slept on a couch in the main room with our rifles handy. It was not long before we were awakened by the sound of the cans rattling and the bells tinkling, as the bear pulled down a caribou front quarter.

I eased over to the window, slid it open and there stood the bear, just underneath the second story east window. Sandy leaned out and fired.

The bear jumped straight up, then tore off into the willows.

But it was plumb dark and we would have to wait for daylight to track the wounded bear through the dense willow thickets surrounding the lodge.

Murphy must have been laughing heartily when later that night an overcast moved in and snow began falling on the hitherto bare ground.

By morning we had six inches of new snow.

This was not a good prospect for locating the bear, but we have to play the hand we're dealt by nature.

Jake, Sandy, Pop, Max and the grizzly.

After a quick breakfast, Sandy, Max, and I started the search. I pointed to the ground where the bear was standing when Sandy shot it, and told Max to "hunt 'em up - go see" was the command, and he excitedly began to nose around, inhaling deeply and occasionally snorting.

Max had an exceptionally fine nose for a Labrador Retriever and he got right on the trail, snow covered or not. With the heavy layer of fresh snow he would occasionally get off track, then retrace his route and get back on the trail, his tail continually wagging with enthusiasm.

It took us about thirty minutes of slow, cautious searching to locate the bear. It was lying bunched up in a small dwarf birch bush, completely covered by new snow and dead as a rock, less than one hundred yards from the lodge.

Sandy, Dave and Pop with the nuisance Grizzly hide.

Sandy's bullet entered the top of the withers and penetrated straight through to the heart. As is commonly the case, the bear went off at full speed for about sixty yards before it dropped, stone dead.

We spent the day skinning and fleshing the hide. It was good to have that dangerously bold cabin bear taken care of - forever.

The next day was decent, so we loaded the cub and I took Sandy back to school.

I doubt that many excused school absences are due to the necessity of a student having to go out into the bush to kill a Grizzly for her Dad, Grandpa, and friends. But this one sure was.

This bear was aged by the Alaska Department of Fish and Game and it was in its tenth year. In my experience the most aggressive, ornery bears are of this age or younger, similar to teenaged boys who want to prove they're the toughest kid in the block.

About a month after our last guests departed, we invited the teacher and his wife over for dinner and gave them the details of Sandy's mission to save us from the aggressive grizzly.

The Rogue Sow

In August of 1989 my knees began to bother me a lot. No specific incident brought it on, but I'd wrenched and twisted both of them many times over the years. Now both knees began making popping noises when I walked. They were painful when I walked and they ached at night while I was lying in bed. And they seemed to be getting worse.

I took care of our four sheep hunters, carrying all the meat, one at a time, along with the heads and capes. Curiously, the heavy loads did not seem to add to my discomfort. Anyway, it was a job that had to be done, but I was curious as well as grateful that packing a heavy load did not add to my discomfort.

For our early September booking period there were four German guest hunters in camp. Three were in their thirties and the other, my good friend Ulrich Herbst was nearly sixty. I was forty-seven and a half years old. Grizzly (*Ursus arctos horribilis*) season opened on September first, so I took two of the younger Germans, my fine Labrador, Max, and an Assistant Guide named Andy, down the valley to the south. I sent a Registered Guide, Lorne, who was in my employ for the season, up the creek to the north with Ulrich and the other German. We four in my group were sitting on a prominence we called the South Overlook when I saw a bear across the valley on the south side of Popple Creek. The bear was maybe three miles from us. It was a medium sized, light colored bear and it was ambling fairly rapidly across the hillside munching on berries as it went.

The young Germans wanted to go after the bear right away. The grizzly was big enough, but I told them that it was moving too fast for us to catch and we would be much better off staying where we were, as we could glass a large area in hopes of finding an even bigger bear. Additionally, I was not motivated by the prospect of struggling through the mile or so of dense, waist high, pucker brush we'd have to transit to get to the bear. However, I kept those considerations to myself.

I had convinced those two young, raring-to-go, "Ubermensch" to remain contentedly in our position when a larger, darker bear showed on that same far hillside and it appeared to be following the first one. Soon the larger bear was chasing after the other. Darn, this meant now I would have to fight my way through all that foot tangling, knee wrenching, pucker brush.

So, we bailed off the South Overlook and began humping and twisting our way through the bushes. We crossed a caribou trail occasionally, but none were going our way, so we were forced to lift our legs high with every step. My knees soon became hot and bothered. And they were noisy - similar to popcorn in a skillet.

We reached the south side of Popple Creek just in time to see the blond bear top out and go over a saddle into the next drainage, with the dark bear close behind. By then they were in sheep country and soon out of sight. Double darn!

I told everyone that now we had virtually no chance of seeing either bear again. So we may as well kick back and eat some lunch. I expected the dark bear to be a rank boar that would eventually catch the smaller sow and likely kill and eat her.

We moved up to a knoll that provided good visibility and started to take out our sandwiches when, to my extreme surprise, the dark bear re-appeared on the ridge and started downhill toward us. I told the fellow with the bear tag, Gunter, to pocket his sandwich as we would go up after that bear, right away. I forgot about my knee discomfort, which in fact, seemed to have disappeared. A bear can be a huge distraction - sometimes for the better.

As we were about to leave, I told my assistant, Andy, to stay put and keep watching the bear. I would be looking back to him for directions. He was to extend his arms right or left to indicate the way we should go, and if he thought we needed to really speed up, he was to so indicate with both arms, straight up and jack them up and down, quickly.

Andy asked, "Jake, what if we see a good moose or caribou, or wolf … or…"

"Andy, if by some unexpected miracle, you should personally witness the second coming of Christ, as we are going up after the bear, please ignore that momentous event until we have finished with that grizzly. I want you to stay totally focused on the bear. Do you understand?" I wanted to make it unequivocally clear.

"Jake, I got it," he confirmed.

The hillside we were climbing had a series of little flats or benches of thirty to forty yards in width. Between the flat spots were steep slopes of twenty to thirty yards from top to bottom. It was a distinctly terraced hillside. Before we were out of sight of the bear due to the grade of the first slope, we saw the bear sit down on on its rump on one of the clumps of grass and sedge. The day was warm and we were all sweaty. Pesky mosquitos and white sox followed us in pestiferous swarms.

A golden eagle swooped by the bear and on the bird's second pass the bear got up and jumped at the eagle. This was one very irritated grizzly!

We lost sight of the bear when we got to the base of the hill, so I told Gunter to put a bullet in the chamber leaving his safety on and replace the round in the magazine. I did the same, which gave each of us four shots, rather than just three. Also, I told him to put his scope on it's lowest power of magnification, as we might suddenly find ourselves very close to this angry bear before shooting it.

"Yah, Jake, but are you going to make film?" he asked.

I was carrying my video camera, a somewhat bulky model that was common in those days before development of high quality mini-cameras, and I told him that I would leave it in it's case until I saw how things were developing.

Max, my Lab, was just to the left and a couple of steps behind me, - "at heel" - as I had trained him to do. Gunter was to my right and a few steps behind me.

The bear had been coming down the main slope, so I expected to find it lower on the main hill than where I had last sighted the bruin. I figured we'd see him sitting or lying, resting in the sunshine on the little plateau between slopes. We cautiously walked up toward the area I calculated it should be.

On my frequent visual checks with Andy, he remained standing with both arms straight up, indicating that we were on course and should continue our route up the slope.

We came to the first bench and eased over the edge as we looked for the bear, but saw nothing. The second bench was the same - devoid of any sign of the bear.

Andy was still indicating we should continue going up the mountainside. As we were going up the slope toward the next bench I became aware of someone screaming back down at the creek. It sounded like someone was panicked or maybe had gotten snake bit. That was a ridiculous thought as there are no snakes in Alaska, but I turned to look back, then caught myself in this foolish move, the like of which has lead to the mauling of several guides. I jerked my head back around and looked uphill to see the big Grizzly coming full speed downhill, fully focused on us at about twenty yards and closing fast.

I hollered at Gunter who was still on my right side and a bit behind. I said "Gunter, shoot!" as I held just beneath the bear's chin and squeezed. Our two shots were simultaneous, Pa-Boom ! I jacked another round in with the bear still coming, and my second bullet also impacted the beast's chest.

"Jake mine wafen doesn't verk," he screamed at me in fear and frustration. Gunter's rifle had jammed.

At extremely close quarters, my dog Max broke for the bear and the dog's action caused the big grizzly to turn to it's right, toward Max. My third shot, a broadside, was a bit aft and high. It broke the bear's pelvis from the left side.

Max and the bear went over the steep edge of the slope into the willows at the edge of the draw and into the creek drainage. They were immediately out of sight.

I was worried that my fine dog might be killed by the bear, but Max came back up over the edge, ears flopping, tongue handing out, and panting noisily. Max was really excited and kept turning to look back toward the bear.

With my last round chambered I approached the edge, as I stuffed three more rounds into the magazine. Then I saw the bear trying to climb up the opposite side and out of the small creek, headed away from us.

Gunter was ready with a new round in his rifle, so I told him to finish the bear. I had my video camera out and running when he fired. His shot hit the bear squarely at the base of the neck and it collapsed.

Max, well pleased, Gunter still gasping, and the rogue sow.

Gunter was open mouthed, gasping for breath, but no sound was coming from him. I filmed his extreme, but silent, excitement. Shortly thereafter he regained his ability to breath and began to relate his perception of the freshly experienced, never to be forgotten incident.

Andy and the other German, Uli, got to us much quicker than we had covered that same distance and Uli was loudly berating me for putting his good friend at such an inordinate risk.

"Jake you are awful guide, mine freund could have been killed, gefallen … " - he would lapse in and out of Deutsch, then back into English, … as he ranted on.

Gunter told him, "Uli, SHUT UP. This is the most exciting day - the most important and favorite day - of my life !"

So Uli abruptly switched his vocal gears and began extolling my expertise and expounding on what a wonderful guide and fellow I was, after all. Germans tend to be very obsequious and defer to the most high ranking in their group. Gunter was the top man of that group.

Calmly Gunter admires his huge female grizzly.

Max was aggressively jabbing the bear with his nose, then coming back to me for a pet and encouragement. My wonderful dog showed his extreme pleasure at the whole deal. I believe he kept me from taking at least a hard impact, and probably a serious mauling.

I got a lot of this on video tape which helped make a ninety minute finished video for the fall season. That longest of all my annual videos sold very well and hundreds of copies were distributed around the world in the NTSC American version, the PAL version used commonly in Europe and the SECAM system used in France. The excited reactions of those two Germans were of particular interest and appeal to viewers.

The first thing we noticed was that the big, well furred Grizzly was a female. Her nipples were fully formed, indicating she had nursed some cubs, but not recently. I guessed she had been without cubs for several years. She was well furred with no noticeable scars and she was in overall in excellent condition. Except now she was dead.

Andy and I took our time skinning the bear. We could see the lodge located five and a half air miles up creek and were already tired, so we fleshed the hide closely to minimize the weight, with which we would have to struggle through the pucker brush in the valley floor before reaching the slippery, stream polished, and mossy rocks of the creek bottom. We brought out the hams of this fat bear.

About half way back to the lodge, Andy did see some caribou, but no second coming of Christ was evident, so not anxious to add weight to our loads, we plugged along without interruption.

At the lodge we were pleased to learn that Ulrich, too, had taken a bear that day. Shortly after I left with my group, he spotted a Grizzly from the kitchen window just across the creek from the lodge. He and Lorne were within easy shooting range in less than half an hour. Ulrich and I had seen a huge dark boar in the same spot in 1986 and Ulrich convinced himself that this was the same bear. But ground shrinkage proved to have been severe. It was not the same large bear we'd seen three years before, but his bear still squared a bit over seven feet.

Gunter's ornery old sow squared just over eight and a half feet, which is about as big as one can expect an interior Grizzly to get and it was the largest sow that I have ever seen. It's skull, too, was much larger than that of most sows. I would have bet heavily on its being a boar, from the look of the head, its behavior, and the overall size of the beast.

That female won second place for that species in the statewide big three contest for grizzlies in 1989. Most sows never place in the top three.

The Alaska Department of Fish and Game removed a vestigial mandibular premolar tooth for aging at the time of sealing. I asked to be informed of the age of the bear.

Several months later I was informed that the sow was twenty-six years of age, which was a special delight for Gunter, as Germans prefer to take old animals, rather than just big ones.

Gunter enjoyed an extremely lucky and satisfying hunt with us, as in addition to his huge grizzly, he took the number one caribou, the number three moose and a fine, old Dall ram with broomed-off horns well past a full curl, but the ram scored just a bit shy of making the top three.

In 2006, while touring Germany with my family, Gunter and his wife drove a long distance to bring me a bottle of wine and spend an afternoon reminiscing about our hunt of seventeen years before. He stated that it was the best hunting experience of his life and remained the best day of his life. I assured him that it was at the top of the list for me, too.

I reckon every one of us that afternoon had been shaken and stirred.

"PULL" Another Bear

In 2007 from mid August until mid September on several occasions we observed a huge male Grizzly around the lodge. After my grandson Spencer shot a caribou on the hills just east of the lodge on August 20, the big bruin soon appeared and fed on the gut pile.

Following his meal of guts a-la-tundra, he lingered on the berry patches easily within shooting range of the lodge, returning regularly to the kill site, apparently in hope of finding more delicious tidbits. But bear season did not open until the first of September and we would have no hunter with a bear permit in camp until the sixth of the month.

In my experience large bears like this one are less inclined to be boldly aggressive than are younger bruins. However they can be persistent. Twice in one day I ran the bear away from the meat pole a few feet from the lodge by shouting from the kitchen window. I cautioned everyone to be especially alert when using the outside privy and every other outdoor activity near the lodge and everywhere else, of course.

One morning in late August I saw the same bear rolling in blue berry patches near the caribou kill site. Then he went back to the spot of his previous meat dinner, apparently checking to see if another serving might be found. Finding only his own droppings and torn up tundra, he ambled off the hills and came toward the lodge. As I fried the bacon for breakfast I keep track of the beast from the window. Suddenly a large grey wolf intersected the bear's trail and turned immediately to follow the bruin at a trot.

After alerting the remaining hunter, Kouros, and my Assistant Guide, Ron Phillips, I took out my video camera and began to film. The two great carnivores were only about two hundred yards from the lodge. We were delighted and entertained to watch the wolf harassing the bear for more than thirty minutes. Repeatedly the lobo would come up behind the bear and when it got within a few feet, the bruin would sense his antagonist's presence and spin around. The wolf would jump back and after several of these scenarios, the bear sat down. He was covering his behind, it seemed. I was reminded of a politician after revelation of his or her inappropriate actions.

As the wolf circled, the huge bear pivoted on its butt to keep the irksome canine in clear sight. The two apex predators performed like heavy weight boxers in a ring. The wolf would jab in close, drawing a counter lurch from the bear. It seemed to be a game for the wolf, providing us with great entertainment and unique video footage. *See this footage on my website: www.huntfish.us/.*

Obviously the old bear was not amused.

Eventually the bear rose and began to amble away, occasionally wheeling around when the wolf approached too closely. After a few hundred yards, the wolf tired of his game and trotted to the caribou kill site. I suspected those animals had endured previous encounters. No doubt each considered himself to be the king of the valley.

We didn't sight the big bear again until mid September. I hosted a husband and wife, Bruce and Lori, who were both drawn for a bear permit, but they wanted to take only one grizzly. I'd told them about the exceptional bear we'd been seeing, and their thoughts were focused on the giant I had described.

Most of the animal traffic in the valley passes within sight of the lodge, so we spent the daylight hours on points of view on the east side of the drainage within a mile of the lodge. The streams were high from rain that week and would be treacherous to cross, so the east side was our best bet from which to watch and the easiest place for us to access. We glassed some average sized bears, but with plenty of time, we decided to hold out for a chance at the big one.

From a favorite glassing point Ron located a band of caribou bulls and after an easy stalk the lady took a good one at about two hundred yards, demonstrating her considerable prowess with the .300 Winchester Magnum she carried. I was confident that she would perform well if given an opportunity at a bear.

Lori and her Caribou bull.

Ron had to go back home to pilot a Boeing 747 for Delta Airlines on a trip to Singapore and other cities, so his departure left just the three of us at the lodge.

One windy day we sat in a relatively sheltered spot from which we could glass up and down Trail Creek. A trickle of caribou here and there in the morning kept us alert but upon close optical scrutiny we located no trophy bulls.

Right at solar midday, which is about half past two o'clock, I saw what at first I thought was the great bear. It was browsing about three and a half miles up creek in a large blue berry patch, across the flooded creek from us. I had left the spotting scope at the lodge that morning and as we watched the animal I convinced myself and my guests that the critter we were seeing was a musk ox, not the bear. After a couple hours of viewing, the wind chill got to us so we decided to head back to the comforts of the lodge. But I began to puzzle about the hairy object of our attention. The "musk ox" had remained in a small open area on the alluvial fan, whereas they normally transit through such terrain and linger longer in the riparian areas near the streams. The situation called for a closer look.

As soon as we entered the lodge I took the tripod mounted, fifteen to sixty power spotting scope to the north window of my bedroom and trained it on the animal. I was humbled to see that the critter was, in fact, a big bear and it was most likely THE big bear! I should have figured that out much earlier, given it's prolonged stay in the open berry patch. I offered a view from the scope to both hunters and told them it was too late to pursue the bear that day and the creeks were high enough to be difficult to impossible to cross anyway, but by morning if we got no more rain, the water level should drop and we might have an opportunity to get after that special bruin.

Apologizing to the hunters, I admitted that I should have recognized the situation much earlier.

As light faded I could still see the animal feeding in the same berry patch.

The welcome morning aroma of coffee brought my guests from their bedroom. Of course their first question was about the bear. The towering mountains that surround the lodge delay the morning light reaching Trail Creek, but once it comes, it increases quickly. As the sun illuminated the valley we all concentrated on the far berry patch, but it revealed nothing. As I turned back to the coffee pot I caught sight of a dark form on the alluvial fan to the west and directly across the creek from the lodge. It proved to be the big bear, ambling toward the large cut bank that outlined the willow choked bottom of the valley. I told Bruce and Lori to get ready quickly as I expected the bear to drop off the cut bank, come through the dense willows and cross the open area of the main runway as it headed back to check the nearly three week-old caribou kill site in the eastern foothills. If the bear stayed the course, we should not have to even cross the main stream.

Having consumed only a cup of coffee, Lori asked if she should whip together some sandwiches for us all. I told her there was no time for that because we had to go immediately to intercept the bear as he walked through the open space. Dropping that heavy bear on the runway would be a wonderful gift. I liked the idea of minimizing the distance I would have to pack that hide, using my new artificial knees which were installed the previous March.

In short order we were standing near the airplane and watching the bear as it approached the cut bank. It sat down on the edge, seemed to deliberate for a few minutes, and then turned back from whence it had come, setting a brisk pace back to the north. There was only a slight breeze from up the valley, so the bear would not have smelled us. I wondered what caused it to so drastically alter its course.

We three went as fast as we could travel to the north west, expecting to reach a point up creek that should put us within reasonable shooting range. When we reached the still flooded creek, I found a braided area that looked crossable. After cutting walking poles for balance and support, we forded the stream, stashing the poles for use on our return. We struggled through the dense willows and climbed up onto the cut bank.

The bear was still walking rapidly through the open tundra about eight hundred yards ahead of us. I expected it to pause to feed on berries it had missed the day before, but the bear kept going. We high stepped and stumbled through the hip wrenching tussocks in pursuit, but the bear did not pause to feed or look back. Our best pace was producing only a marginal gain on the bruin.

After more than an hour of maximum effort we had passed the site where we observed the bear the day before and still were approximately two hundred and fifty yards from our quarry. In a few minutes the bear would enter a dense stand of willows, cottonwoods, and alders and likely be lost to us. Normally I would have the hunter put off attempting a shot until we were closer, but Bruce had hunted with me many times since his first trip in 1978 and I knew that he shot exceptionally well. Lori had proved her shooting ability days before on her caribou. I told them that we were as close as we would ever be and they should shoot before the bear got across the last open stretch of tundra. I expected the bear to take a bullet, then slow down, maybe even roll around, as he fought whatever he figured had bitten him. This would give the shooters an excellent opportunity for more shots, and to finish him off in the open.

The shooting began, but the bear continued in his rapid walk, never breaking into a run and never showing sign of being hit or bothered in the least. In all, ten shots were carefully fired by those two competent marksmen with none finding their target. The huge grizzly disappeared into the willows, untouched.

I was literally shellshocked, as were Bruce and Lori. I couldn't believe several of the unexpected events of that morning. My guests sat on the tundra, heads down and dejected.

I was reminded of a Snoopy cartoon.

As I continued to watch the willow patch, a second bear came rushing out of the brush from near the point of entry of the first bear and ran straight toward us. This was a good sized grizzly, but a bit smaller and lighter in color than the first. The animal continued at a full lope toward us. It was as if someone had said "Pull" for another clay pigeon to be launched.

"Hey, look, here comes another one and this is no small bear either," I told my dejected friends. They lifted their heads unenthusiastically.

"Hunker down and get ready. Fill your barrel and magazine, cuz he's coming right to us, and he's a good one," I urged. With adrenaline induced vigor they loaded up.

The blonde Grizzly glanced behind several times, then slowed down as he started up the slight grade toward our position.

Apparently comfortable that the larger bear was not following him, the second bear began to feed on blue berries.

We stayed frozen in place. Actually we were all sweaty from our prolonged efforts to get within range of the first bear. I kept easing my head up and stealing glimpses of the bear as it worked its way uphill and closer to us. A steady, gentle wind from the north calmed my concerns that the bear might catch our scent.

At sixty yards I whispered to Lori to raise up to see the bear and shoot as soon as she was ready. "Hold dead-on for what you want to hit. Aim just below the chin if he is looking at you!"

Balanced on one knee she fired and dropped the bear in its tracks.

The stillness of the valley was interrupted by whoops of joy from all of us. This was indeed a trophy boar Grizzly. Later at the lodge, it would measure right at seven and a half feet on the square. The beautiful hide was tinged with blonde and had no sign of rub marks or scars. I estimated its age at between ten and twelve years.

The thee of us set about skinning the beast, frequently looking up to see if the larger bear might appear, but we saw no more of the giant.

Lori with her dandy boar Grizzly.

My bilateral complete knee replacement had been done just six months before, but I tied the hide with head and feet attached on my pack board and slowly lugged it the four and a half air miles (more like double that distance through the boggy tundra and brush) while Bruce carried the hams and Lori toted most of the rest of our stuff. We spent nearly three hours on the return trip. We hit the river right where we'd cached our poles for crossing the rapidly flowing stream, which was very helpful to all of us in our tired state and laden with our weighty burdens. It had a been a long day without any food except for the one cup of coffee and some bits of nut and candy snacks from Lori's pack. But it was a very good day.

As a big supper of caribou, spuds, canned corn and blue berry crisp cooked, we recalled the events of the day. I have no explanation for why the big bear suddenly decided to turn and head north at such a rapid pace. Nor could any of us could explain how two such good shooters, using balanced rests for their rifles, had missed multiple times, even though the range was a bit long. But misses happen to the best of them at times and that's just one of those inexplicable things.

The second bear was a stranger to me, having never seen him before he came barreling out of the brush. I reckon he was new to the area, but acquainted with the big boy, which was obviously the dominant bear. Most likely the second bear was startled by the rapid approach of the larger one and panicked, which brought him right to us, nearly into our laps.

The sound of rifle shots seems to have little effect, if any, on game in the area. Both bears had no doubt heard the shooting, but were not bothered by it, as similar noises from rocks tumbling down the sides of the valleys is an everyday occurrence.

Bruce and Lori wanted to skin out the head and feet and flesh the hide the next day, so I cleaned up the lodge and took inventory on food and supplies needed for the coming year. Bruce prepared a tasty bear stew that evening and the next night we had a feed of fresh snowshoe hare. On the last day in camp Bruce took an ancient bull caribou.

We never saw that giant grizzly again that season.

In December of 2008 we learned that Lori's caribou placed third in the APHA/SCI statewide competition and our other guests of 2007 took the number one and the number two caribou and the number two wolf. Her bear just missed the number three trophy for grizzlies. It had been a good season for all of us.

A Toklat Grizzly in Heavy Snow

In 1991 we had an eight inch snowfall in late August. The temperature remained below freezing and subsequent low pressure fronts kept dumping more of the white stuff. Aufis glaciers were forming in all branches of the river and creeks, and the ice was growing relentlessly as the days wore on.

Aufis refers to ice that forms in shallow streams. After the first layer of ice forms, overflow on top of that layer then freezes and the ice increases in thickness if cold temperatures persist. We have measured Aufis glaciers near the lodge that were more than seven feet thick.

The snow, early and in earnest, was likely the stimulus that brought large numbers caribou in herds ranging from dozens to hundreds or thousands, off the north slope and down Trail Creek as they headed for their winter range several hundred miles to the south.

As for the grizzlies, the sows with cubs denned early that year and some, especially those with very young cubs, did not emerge. That was most likely due to their den temperature remaining below freezing so the bears did not get wet in their beds.

I've observed that when a bear gets wet in its den, it will come out, walk around as the moisture on their coat freezes, while the interior of the opened den also freezes. Shortly thereafter the bears roll to rub off the ice formed on their guard hairs. Then, often the same day, they go back into their icy dens and usually remain content in their winter shelters until spring unless they get wet again. A hibernating bear does fine for months in a frozen den, but if it becomes wet, the bear will wake up and get out into the fresh air. This applies to all ages and both sexes of bears from young sows with cubs to ancient boars. I've seen this often in grizzlies, but have not observed it in black bears. The high population of grizzlies probably is responsible for the lack of black bears on Trail Creek. I last saw a black bear in that country in 1978. The grizzlies just ate 'em up, I guess.

Old boars tend to go to their dens, or make a new one, later than younger bears. In spite of the considerable snow cover, it hadn't become really cold at Trail Creek and the resident mature boars were out and about, drawn by the increased caribou traffic.

Several rutty bull moose were cruising north, then turning around and walking south - looking for love or a fight. The bulls were searching for cows, and on Trail Creek each year they traipse up and down the drainage throughout the rutting season, which begins in the middle of September and continues until about the middle of October in that latitude.

The bears' natural drive to add as much weight as possible before winter sets in compels them to consume as much food as possible, with fat and protein from large mammals at the top of the list. Bears are wired that way. Any possibility of a moose or caribou kill is an irresistible enticement to them.

Bear success in taking moose, especially large bull moose in the fall, is much higher than catching caribou. The big bulls often bed down in the brush, being tired after spending a lot of time and effort searching, breeding, fighting with other bulls, and eating very little. This makes them especially vulnerable to predation by bears.

Bears rarely caught caribou as the tundra deer crossed through the willows close to the stream. Nevertheless, seeing caribou anywhere, even in the relative safety of open country, drew and held the bears' attention.

In September of 1991, my concrete contractor friend, Lloyd was among our guests. Lloyd had taken a couple of big moose with me, one by rifle and the second by bow. He'd taken several bears of different species, including a grizzly, and he was looking for something special. With bear hunters, "special" usually means either an enormous animal or one that is strikingly different in color or markings. The booking was for fourteen days, so we did not feel rushed.

Everyday we were distracted by the massive movements of Barren Ground caribou of the Western Arctic Herd. Some of the animals lingered a bit as they slogged south through the snow, but most kept on a steady march.

The local grizzlies were even more distracted by the tundra deer than we were, although most adult bears learn early that chasing caribou over open ground is not apt to be successful in providing fresh meat.

The bears frequently provided us with interesting glassing through our "long eye" lenses. We did see two different young bears charging across open tundra areas in attempts of run down a caribou, but we noticed no older bruins engaging in such ineffective adventures. With plenty of game and seemingly sufficient time we observed and rejected several single bears as they exerted themselves in strenuous efforts to secure some fresh meat.

One afternoon I returned to the lodge with a hunter from a four-day, and successful, moose pursuit just as my long time friend, Jim Cann, was about to set off to try to get within reasonable shooting distance of a bear that Lloyd had decided would fill the bill as that "special" one he was after.

Lloyd and Jim paused to put the big lodge telescope on the bruin for me to observe. The bear had positioned itself on the snowy slope of a large bluff in the foothills across the river from the lodge. This bear was a large one with Toklat markings, the like of which is more common on Trail Creek than most places in Alaska. Most such colored grizzlies are female, but this one had size enough and was not accompanied by cubs, so it was potentially a boar and in any event, it was a dandy candidate for the wizardly magic of a taxidermist to change it into a parlor bear - whether its anatomy included a rudder or not.

Early that same morning I got out of the tent and saw that the margins of the lake I was on with my float plane had frozen solid, with open water in the middle, but about forty yards from shore. I probed the ice near shore and stabbed through just less than three inches of solidified water. We struck the tent, loaded up and were ready to vacate the area. I sat on the bow of the right float and broke ice ahead with a paddle. It was slow going, so the hunter sat on the other float and helped break ice. We spent over an hour in our uncomfortable, contorted positions before we reached water to take off. We both were tuckered out.

Jim had spotted the grizzly a half hour before I landed, and I was tired from my three cold nights in a tent and the unusually demanding morning activities, so when he asked if I wanted to do the stalk I told him to just

ALASKA BEARS Stirred and Shaken

Lloyd with his very "special" bear.

This large Toklat grizzly was a boar of about ten years of age.

go ahead. He'd been guiding longer that I had, but he had not been involved with taking a bear so far that season.

After getting out of my hip boots, grabbing a fresh oatmeal cookie and pouring a cup of coffee I monitored Lloyd and Jim's progress as they maneuvered toward the bear. The big tripod mounted telescope in the warm lodge made it all clear and very comfortable.

The pair of hunters climbed up the big cut bank which lined the river. Once on top, they found a gully they could sneak up, out of sight of the bear. Their stalk put them half way to the the prominence where the bear was resting.

As they worked their way toward the bear, using every bit of the sparse cover available, they stopped about two hundred yards from the unsuspecting predator. Then they worked their way through an ice and snow cluttered rocky cliff to put themselves downwind, but still downhill from the bear.

A string of a couple dozen caribou passed below the hunters and the grizzly. This movement of potential fresh groceries brought the bear to its feet and it began to slowly move down the hill toward a lower bench. But the caribou passed too quickly for his stalk. The bear sat on its rump, then stretched out on its belly, watching for another opportunity.

With the bear in its new position, Jim and Lloyd could approach the hill unseen by their quarry and they hustled toward a position that would put them slightly uphill from their target.

Slowly the two men made their way through the snow covered, icy rocks and after a few minutes they were within eighty yards of the placid bear.

Lloyd didn't want to shoot the critter in its bed, so Jim hollered and the bear stood up on all fours, looking in the direction of the sound.

Lloyd put a bullet into the chest of the grizzly. It dropped straight away and did not move again. Lloyd had his special grizzly.

From my warm, comfortable seat at the table, sipping on a mug of coffee, I gave a big whoop when the bear went down. This was a bear hunt the like of which I had never before experienced. I enjoyed the whole show, but not nearly so much as if I'd been along on the stalk.

Feeling guilty, I went out and sawed up some willows and alders for the sauna stove while Jim and Lloyd tended to the skinning and packing the hide and all four quarters back to the lodge. Compared to most, this was an easy pack back to the lodge.

The caribou kept coming off the North Slope and right down Trail Creek for another two weeks, but we did not see another grizzly to compare with the dandy taken by Lloyd.

MARCH, 2017

As I review this book prior to sending it off for printing and distribution in April, 2017, the stories spark my anticipation and enthusiasm for next fall's hunts in the Arctic.

2017 marks my fiftieth year of hunting bears and other wild and free game in Alaska, and though most of my time and effort has been directed at guiding and helping others to make their dreams come true, the memories that I am left with are ever present and sustain my appreciation for how truly blessed I am.

Of one thing I am sure, I will never tire of the grand endeavor - the pursuit of big game, whether to photograph or harvest.

So let's all sharpen our rifles, make ready our cameras, and prepare for the hunt!

Jake Jacobson
Alaska Master Guide #54

All of Jake's books are available through Amazon.com & other book sellers - OR signed copies can be ordered directly from Jake.

www.ingramcontent.com/pod-product-compliance
Lightning Source LLC
Chambersburg PA
CBHW071710160426
43195CB00012B/1639